WHAT TO

BUYING
OR
SELLING A
HOUSE

WHAT TO WATCH OUT FOR WHEN

BUYING

OR

SELLING

A

HOUSE

by

MICHAEL LLEWELYN

PAPERFRONTS

ELLIOT RIGHT WAY BOOKS
KINGSWOOD, SURREY.

Set in 10pt Times. Printed and bound in Great Britain by Cox & Wyman Ltd, Reading.

CONTENTS

AUTHOR'S NOTE

This book falls into two parts. Chapters One to Nine deal with the problems of buying a house, while chapters Ten to Sixteen deal with selling, mainly on a 'do-it-yourself' basis.

Knowing that there will be those who buy the book in order to read the selling section, I have deliberately written it with them in mind, but this does mean that there is an inevitable degree of repetition. I hope the readers who start at the beginning will excuse this.

The whole area of home ownership has changed in a number of ways since I first wrote this book. New approaches to mortgage policy; encouragement of home ownership by Government; the end of strict fee scales required by the various professional advisers; all have led to change and new initiatives which the householder ought to understand, whether he is buying or selling.

It is for this reason that I have been delighted to co-operate and extend the usefulness I hope this book has provided by bringing up-to-date this new edition.

INTRODUCTION

Mankind needs four things to ensure his survival: Air, water, food and shelter. For most of us, in this country, the first two present few problems, although some steps have become necessary, recently, to keep our supplies of both reasonably pure.

The vast majority of us get enough to eat. Many other countries are less fortunate, in this respect, but they do share our particular weakness. Shelter.

Many of our fellow countrymen may never enjoy decent living conditions.

Several years in the property business have shown me that the operation of a free market in house prices means that it is extremely difficult for those of slender means to buy a house of their own. Equally, the last seventy years have shown that tinkering with the problem simply makes it worse. Ointment has failed and surgery seems the only answer. I suspect that many other people think the same; not all of them of left wing political views, either.

On the other hand, I believe that a person should have a home and that he should be able to own it, if he chooses. The two views are not incompatible.

A complex economic situation is bad enough, but for the average home seeker, the legal and practical problems facing him only serve to make the situation worse.

You need practical advice, in such circumstances and that is the aim of this book. To explain the problems, to give you the alternatives and to help you find your best course in what must seem a morass of difficulties and hazards.

At the same time, it is hoped that you will also learn how to do for yourself, as much of the donkey work of home ownership as is reasonable.

The success of my attempt will be measured only by your success in this difficult field.

MICHAEL LLEWELYN

1

The Background to the Problem

Future historians will probably call this the 'Home Ownership Age'. At no time has there been so much discussion of the problems of providing homes for all. For that matter, there have probably never been so many problems facing those who wish to set up home for themselves.

Of course, all those newspaper advertisements give the impression that there are no problems, at all. Dozens of properties appear, day after day, all set out in enticing splendour, by experts who know just how to attract the home seeker's eye.

Builders claim that 'you should buy your new home from them'. Estate Agents offer 'homes for sale', hinting that to buy from anyone else means that your 'home' will be substandard – not a proper home at all.

All this is rubbish. No one can sell, lease or rent you, a 'home'. A home is something that is created from your contentment; the place where you relax and enjoy your family. Only you can make a 'home'. All that the builder can sell you is a house – or a bungalow, or a flat.

So, as a first warning; never be fooled into believing that only maximum expense will get you a home. Expense has nothing to do with it. There are couples who have made homes in two attic rooms which have pulsated with joy, while others have failed to find happiness in marble halls.

Primitive man had few house problems. He built his shelter where he wished, and pretty squalid it was. As time went by, however, richer, more powerful people began to build bigger and more impressive houses.

Probably, the most splendid 'house' of all is Versailles, the palace built by the King of France, some two hundred years ago. Its splendour beggars description. Room after magnificent room – hundreds of them, and not a water pipe, a sewer pipe or a lavatory in the place. Splendid squalor, as opposed to the sordid squalor in which ordinary people lived.

The idea of owning one's own house is quite a new one, for the average man. Our remote ancestors were probably like the Red Indians who had no real conception of 'owning' land. You could own your tepee, perhaps, but land was land. No one owned it – everyone could use it.

This is why the Indians did not really object to the first Americans – until they realized their totally different outlook, and by then, it was too late.

This vague idea is all very well when man is a hunter and there is plenty to hunt. Mobility is essential and his roots never go very deep. In any case, he probably only stayed in one place until he had so fouled the site that even he could no longer stand the smell.

As man became a planter and farmer, he began to object to other people helping themselves to his crops and the idea of 'ownership' of land began to enter his mind. With the growth of tribal organization came chiefs and the concept developed that the Chief 'owned' the tribal land and 'lent' it to his tribesmen. They, in turn, repaid him with part of their crops.

This was essential, as society became more complicated. The Chief was needed to organize the defence of the Tribe and to administer justice within it. He could not do this if he had to spend part of his time on his own land, in order to feed his family. By receiving part of everyone else's produce, he could be a full-time Chief.

All this reached its most organized level in the Feudal System of the Middle Ages. The ideas behind this were very simple.

Essentially, all land belonged to God and he lent it to the King. As the King was also the spokesman of God, the Almighty usually got the rough end of the bargain, while the King did very nicely by 'lending' the land, in parcels, to his chief followers.

They became the Aristocracy and, in turn, 'lent' their land to lesser nobles, down a widening pyramid, until we find the local Knight lending out, at an acre or so a time, to the serfs who actually cultivated it.

Everyone paid for his land by handing over part of his crop, by working so many days on his 'lord's' land and by serving as a soldier in his lord's army, when required.

Essentially, the system was one of barter and bartering has one great disadvantage, despite the enthusiasm of those who support it, even now. It lacks elasticity. There were other problems. When the Sun shone, the serf wanted to harvest his crop. So did the Lord of the Manor. Unfortunately, the serf was supposed to harvest his lord's crops, as part of his 'service rent'. In the rugged, brutal society that was England, six hundred years ago, it is fairly obvious whose crop was harvested and whose was spoiled.

Inevitably, like all systems that did not really deliver the goods, the Feudal System ground itself into the mud. Instead of service, or crops, Landlords began to accept cash, and the modern concept of renting began.

The importance of this development can be seen, today, in a number of ways. Firstly, the aristocratic basis of land-owning is still part of our thinking; we still feel that to own land is somehow respectable and suggests social status for the house owner.

Also, long after the Feudal System ended, the idea has remained firmly in people's minds, that ordinary people – that is you and me – should accept our lot as 'borrowers' of houses and pay rent.

Until the beginning of the First World War, few people in Britain owned the houses in which they lived. Most people rented property and felt that this was an entirely acceptable way of providing their families with accommodation.

The beginning of the change came in the nineteen twenties. This was a period when money became worth much less. An income of five hundred pounds per annum, in 1910, was a princely sum. You could afford to keep a servant on it. By 1925, it was adequate to keep you in modest circumstances and very little more. Of course, many people existed on far less.

Pressed for cash, people owning rented houses, began to sell them, with vacant possession, when the opportunity arose. Increased legislation, which protected tenants from eviction, and kept rents down at an uneconomic level for the landlord, simply added more reason to get your money out of houses and into more attractive investments.

This led to a reduction in the number of rented houses and more and more people found it necessary to consider the possibility of buying, rather than renting. They were helped by the rapid growth of the Building Society movement.

A hundred years ago, you only borrowed money by mortgaging your house, when you had gambled, drunk or otherwise roistered away your money. If the Victorians are to be believed, you borrowed from someone who was always called Sir Jasper and who demanded enormous interest, culminating in the hand of your fair and innocent daughter.

Fed on that sort of propaganda, it is small wonder that people regarded a mortgage as the ultimate in shame; a millstone round the neck of the improvident. It took a long time to replace this view with a more modern idea, that mortgages are a means of buying a house, out of income.

But the idea grew, as the Building Societies grew, and became accepted as responsible, public spirited bodies, quite different from the old 'Sir Jasper' image. The situation has now turned full circle. The average man now expects to buy his house and would be surprised at the suggestion that he should rent.

It is only reasonable, therefore, to make another point.

There is no shame in renting. It is simply another way of providing a family with a house. Many people find that it suits their particular circumstances better than buying; and it is as easy to make a home in a rented house, as in one which you have bought.

And so we find that anyone seeking to set up home, faces a choice. Rent or buy? This is only the first decision of many, as he soon discovers.

The grim fact is, that buying a house is a far more complex matter than almost anything else which the average man ever has to do. This is not really surprising, when you think about it.

A house is the most expensive thing that you will ever own. It will involve you in legal complications, well beyond your ordinary experience, and is usually built in such a way that most of the faults in its construction are well out of sight to all but expert eyes.

And now, the experts appear; all offering to help and guide you; for a fee, of course; through the various complications – Solicitors, Architects, Insurance men, Estate Agents, Builders, to name only the most obvious.

Now it would be wickedly unfair, not to say libellous, to suggest that the vast majority of these professionals are anything other than honest, competent men, trying to earn a living and genuinely provide a proper service to the public. It would be equally silly to suggest that every one of them was a Saint.

Unfortunately, the problem is not just a question of avoiding the obvious villain. Many house owners show remarkably little understanding of the role of the professional man. Normally he is a personable, polite sort of person and the man-in-the-street can easily form the impression that his interests are well safeguarded by such a charming fellow. They may well be, but you should always be sure just who the Professional is actually working for. You, or someone else.

The problem is fairly straightforward, in the case of a Solicitor or an Architect. They are usually working for you, and both you and they know that you will be paying them a fee, in due course. In addition, you have the protection that both Solicitors and Architects are strictly controlled by law. You can seek indemnity from their Professional societies, if they let you down.

On the other hand, when you first come into contact with the Estate Agent, or the Builder, they are usually working for someone else. The Estate Agent is acting for the seller of the house which you are interested in and the Builder is acting for himself.

Once again, please do not assume that each of these gentlemen is trying to steal the shirt off your back. They are most unlikely to try anything so crude. Unfortunately, the line between making the best profit possible and doing you in the eye is very difficult to define, and the innocent house purchaser is much more likely to get the worst of any such encounter. This being so, it is only fair that someone gives you just that bit of guidance that will help you to understand what is happening and will warn you when things are not going as they should.

A little knowledge is not always a dangerous thing. It can be a valuable way of protecting yourself.

2

First Considerations

Is buying a house what you really want to do?

Having just bought a book which, inevitably concentrates on the problems of the owner-occupier, it is probable that you have already decided – yes, to that question. Why? you may ask, should we want to go over the question again.

For the simple reason that few people really know all the essential questions and, in such a situation, one can hardly expect them to come up with the right answers.

Today we are so conditioned to the idea of house owner- ship that it seems almost sacrilegious to suggest that it is really only one way of putting a roof over your family's head: that there are other ways.

While you are getting over that surprise, here is another. It may be that buying a house is not the answer for you. There could be better alternatives.

We have all heard the argument. 'Paying rent', we are told, 'is a waste of money'. You will never own the house, no matter how long you pay. Owning your own house is better. It means that you don't have to pay out, each week.

Unfortunately, this argument is based on a complete mis- understanding of just what rent, and property ownership, actually entail.

A man, seeking a house, has three choices. He can borrow a house from someone else, and pay rent for the right to live in it; he can raise a loan and use it to buy a house, and pay interest on the loan; or, he can buy a house, using his own money, in which case, he gives up the interest which he would have made if he invested the money, instead.

So you see that everyone 'pays' a regular sum, out of his income, for the privilege of living in a house. This is the case, whether he pays it as rent or as interest.

On the other hand, he is not 'spending' any of his money. If he rents a house this is quite obvious. If he buys, he is merely changing his capital from one form of wealth – that is, cash – into another form – property.

If he gives up the house, he reconverts his capital from property into cash. Even if he borrowed the money, in the first place, he just pays back the amount due and is back where he started.

It is quite obvious that, over the last few years, property has tended to go up in value faster than general inflation. As a result, changing property back into cash, after a few years, has generally meant that you finished up with more cash than you started. This sounds marvellous but, of course, it is only so if the money will actually buy more than it would before you bought the house. That is, if you have made a profit in what is usually called 'real terms'.

It must be admitted that the tendency, since the Second World War, has been for people to do just that. This is obviously an incentive to buy, but does anyone benefit? The majority of people, selling a house, are moving to another. They need all that beautiful 'profit' to buy their next house. As this will almost certainly have gone up in price, at the same rate, it is clear that there is no real profit, at all. It is, in the words of the economists, 'Monopoly Money'.

The other point to remember is that there is no divine law that says the process must always be an upward one. Values could come down. History teaches that there have been periods when this has happened.

If that tends to put you off the idea of property owning, do not let it. If you leave your money in pound coins, it will certainly come down in real value. Stocks and shares are just as likely to go down, as up. Property has, for centuries, proved to be the one place where values tend to rise and where your capital is safest.

Most of us would be happy if property simply maintained its value, so that people, wishing to move, could do so without loss. In fact, the rise has been so much faster than the general level of inflation, that the position has become terribly distorted. It is all very well for those who have already bought. They are now on the merry-go-round and can move about to their heart's content. Those not yet on it find that it becomes harder and harder to get on, as it goes faster.

In short, no one benefits, in real terms, from house price

inflation. On the contrary, more and more people are suffering from it.

And so, as you see, we have opened up, once again, the whole question of whether you should rent or buy. Is it quite as straightforward a decision as you thought? Let us go back to basics and start again.

Firstly, what are the relative advantages and dis-advantages of the two alternatives.

A hundred years ago that was quite obvious. An owner lived in his house and could not be put in the street. He knew how much his outgoings were likely to be and could plan his finances accordingly. The tenant, on the other hand, could be thrown out, at the whim of the Landlord. He could also find his rent increased at any time that the Landlord chose. Not only could – far too frequently, did.

Things are much less clear-cut, today.

Society – that is you and me – require a whole range of services from the Government and we seem to want more and more, as time goes by. For this reason, the Government has had to adopt methods of buying compulsorily those properties which are essential for the provision of the services but which the owners do not wish to sell.

The principle is that you should be properly and fully compensated for your loss but it does mean the old idea that, if you owned your own house, you were safe from eviction, is no longer the case.

Tenants, on the other hand, have now much more protection than they used to have. In the nineteenth century the population of our cities exploded, and the demand for more houses grew with it. This had, in the early days, several effects.

Great areas of land were rapidly developed with small, unattractive houses. People realized that uncontrolled development was ruining the environment and that the houses themselves were of poor construction. They began to press Parliament for some control. This was granted, in due course, but, inevitably, it reduced the number of houses being built.

With shortage came increases of cost and the rents of existing houses soared up. People who could not pay were bundled out and replaced by others, who could.

Once again Parliament stepped in with controls; this time in the form of restrictions on the rental that could be charged and specific requirements which must be met before tenants could be evicted.

Generally speaking, this is still the position. If a Landlord wishes to evict you, he must have the permission of the Courts, before he does so. The Court will require a pretty convincing case before it agrees: e.g. the tenant has misbehaved or the Landlord or his family need to live in the property.

This, of course, has done nothing to increase the number of houses available for renting and has, therefore, resulted in the one great disadvantage of rented property.

There isn't any. Or so you may feel, if you go and look.

It is easy to blame Parliament for causing the situation. Just think of the alternative, if there was no planning law, no controls to prevent jerry-building and no restrictions on rent. The injustices caused could be far worse than those we face at present.

We can see what would have happened when we look back at the market in furnished property, before the 1974 Rent Act. There was no control, or restriction over the letting of furnished houses or flats. As a result, what was available came in two basic types.

There was the pleasant house, whose owner planned to be away for six months, or so, and who let it, until he returned to occupy it himself. This was often expensive and was obviously never more than a short-term answer, for any tenant. There was no 'security of tenure' – as it is called – and the best that could be said was that you at least knew when the day of reckoning would come and could plan accordingly.

The 1974 Rent Act extended some protection to furnished tenants but no protection is given where the landlord himself lives in part of the house or intends to return to it and live in it again, in due course.

In fact, if you are only going to be living in an area for a short time, say a year or so, a furnished letting of this type is certainly better than buying and selling again, only a few months later. The profit in such a short time may not cover the costs of selling.

The other sort of furnished property is that which is let,

usually in flats, by the property owner, as an investment. Standards vary from the nice old lady who lets the 'upstairs' of her house; down to the villains who furnish a semi-derelict house with the contents of the local scrap yard, and then attempt to charge high rents to people, desperate for somewhere to live.

As you have already read, no protection has been given to the tenant who shares a house with the dear old lady but it has been given to the tenant of the alternative. In practice, he is probably the one who needs it most.

Fortunately for him, the tenant can now apply to the Rent Officer for a fair rent to be registered if he feels his Landlord is charging too high a rent.

The problem is, of course, that the provision of such protection for furnished tenants results in a growing shortage of that sort of accommodation, over a period of time.

Nowadays, tenants have been granted the same rights whether they live in furnished or in unfurnished property. Consult your local Rent Officer, Housing Aid Centre, or Citizens Advice Bureau for further information.

But you have already decided to buy, or you know that such rented property that there is, in your area, is just too awful to consider. Are you in a position to do so?

Before all else, this must be a matter of finance. Have you got, or can you raise enough?

In practice, the majority of people, in regular employment, can raise a mortgage. The problem is whether it is going to be enough to pay for the house you desire, or, for that matter, any house at all.

For this reason, this is the appropriate time for another word of warning.

Do your sums before you look at any property at all.

Every Estate Agent has met the couple who believe that they have found their dream house. They radiate the indescribable wonder of it all. They reply to his questions through a haze of happiness.

And every Estate Agent has been forced, in too many cases, to smash their dream to bits. The reason? They cannot afford it. They have hopelessly over-estimated just what, in the end, they would be able to pay.

Usually, they go away and come to terms with the position, but only after a great deal of bitter disappointment. Something for which they usually, quite unjustly, blame the poor old Estate Agent.

In fact, it is not difficult to find out exactly what you can afford.

In every town you will find the local offices of one, or more, of the National Building Societies. Their names are so well known from their advertisements that you are bound to recognize them.

The Building Society movement is non-profit making and was set up to enable people to buy houses, for their own occupation. In fact, they are really a form of charitable trust, but that does not mean that they will lend money to you willy-nilly. Apart from anything else, that would not be in your interests. Sooner or later, you have to pay the money back. If you have borrowed more than you can afford, then you will be in trouble, and so will the Building Society.

In order to avoid this, the Societies lay down rules, limiting the amount which they will lend. You will find that most Societies will consider lending you a sum up to eighty per cent of the value of the house. They may lend more, if you take out an insurance policy to provide security for the extra.

Appendix Two, at the end of this book, gives you an indication of just what this means, for the purpose of your first consideration of the problem. However, Societies vary and you will only find out the true position by asking. More about that, later.

The repayment, usually made monthly, consists of the interest due on the loan, plus some capital to reduce the loan. Each year, that little bit of capital repaid means that the actual loan is less, and, as you pay the same total amount, each year, the amount of interest due also goes down, while the capital repaid goes up. Of course, this also means that, in the first few years of the mortgage, the sum outstanding is reduced very slowly and very little. This is always difficult to explain to house owners. They feel that they have paid a great deal of money to the Society. Why has the loan not gone down more than that, they ask?

Well, now you know.

Remember these points. They are important, in two respects, which will be made plainer, at a later stage.

For the moment, let us return to the immediate problem. What can you afford to pay?

The Manager and Staff, at the average Building Society are helpful and understanding to the newcomer to house purchase. Perhaps more important is the fact that they have nothing to gain by telling you anything other than the truth. You can approach them for their advice without fear.

Of course, everyone has an off day, occasionally, but if you are unlucky and find an unhelpful Society, do not be put off. Go to another Society.

Select one of the Societies which are represented in your town, call round and tell the person on the counter that you would appreciate some advice on house purchase. Someone will be found to help you.

Be honest with him. He will ask you just what you earn, and how much deposit you can put down, out of your own money. If you refuse to tell him, then he cannot help you, and, if you exaggerate, you are only hurting yourself. When you actually apply for a mortgage, in due course, the Society will check your claims with your employer.

In calculating just how much you can find from your own savings, always remember that there will be costs which you will have to meet. Appendix Two sets out, roughly, what these are likely to be. You must take these into account and be sure that the necessary sum is left on one side.

You need never worry about the Building Society Manager telling anyone else your private business. He interviews several people like you every day, and it is unlikely that he even remembers the details. Even if he was tempted, the Societies take a very strict view of employees who fail to maintain total secrecy about their customers' affairs.

He will tell you just what you can borrow and, by adding to it the sum which you have available – usually called the deposit, the wrong name but the one which everyone understands – he can also tell you the top price which you can afford to pay, IF YOU BORROW FROM HIS SOCIETY.

This is important. The variations in the way in which Societies apply their rules may mean that another Society will lend you more.

It is extremely unlikely that you will not have at least a rough idea of the price of the type of house which you hope to buy, and you will now know just how your finances measure up to it. If they are adequate then your problems are very nearly at an end.

If, on the other hand, you can only afford a lower price, then you must examine one or two further possibilities.

First of all, ask the Manager if he has calculated the amount over the longest term possible, for your age. This will often reduce the payments slightly and increase the amount which you can borrow.

Secondly, ask if the Society takes into account any or all of a partner's income. Some do, some do not, but it does no harm to ask. In any case, even if he cannot do so, he may know of a Society which does. Competition between Societies has not yet reached the point where he would not advise you of one. Again, it does no harm to ask.

There is no reason why you should not inquire at several Societies and compare results. You could contact the Local Council. It might lend money on mortgage. Councils' rules sometimes differ from those of the Building Societies. They may accept the second income in the calculations and may frequently lend money for the purchase of property which the Building Societies might not accept.

You should understand that a mortgage is a loan for which property is the security. In other words, the property is the valuable item which shows the lender that you have a means of paying back the loan, should the actual cash have been spent.

The ownership of the property stays with the borrower but the Deeds – those papers which prove ownership – are handed over to the lender. If the loan is not repaid, the lender can sell the house, proving his right to do so by showing that the Deeds are in his possession. He would then be required to deduct what is owed to him, from the sale proceeds, and pass the balance on to the borrower.

A Building Society differs in that the loan is used to buy the house which then becomes the security, for the loan. Obviously, if the house is to be the security, the Society will wish to be sure that it will sell for at least the amount outstanding, should the borrower let them down. For this reason, they will have it valued and given a basic structural survey.

You will be required to pay for this survey, even if it results in the Society turning your application down. The Valuer will have done his work and he will want to be paid, whatever the result.

Until 1980 the purchaser never saw the survey report, even though he had paid for it. This was always a source of annoyance amongst purchasers but, in any case, was to be changed by what surveyors now refer to as the 'Yianni Case' – usually with bated breath.

Mr. Yianni bought a house which, without his knowledge, had serious structural faults. Unfortunately, he only required a small mortgage and the Building Society, aware that his loan was well secured, lent him the money. The surveyor had not gone into detail about the defects in his report, no doubt thinking that, as the report was for the Building Society, and the loan was fully secured, even allowing for the defects, they were not important.

As it happened, the defects were more serious than anyone realized and Mr. Yianni decided to sue the surveyor for failing to tell him of the problems. Everyone, including me, expected him to lose his case on the basis that the survey had not been done for him anyway. The Society might have had a case against the surveyor but they had not lost any money.

In fact, the Court upended every surveyor's view of the law, holding that, as Mr. Yianni had paid for the survey, he was entitled to be told of its contents and to sue if faults had not been pointed out to him.

Since that decision, surveyors have been much more wary when surveying for Building Societies.

If the Valuer thinks that the loan will not be covered by the value, the Society will usually make you an offer of less than you asked for. In such a case, you will either have to find the balance for yourself, or ask the Vendor to reduce the price of the house.

Another word of warning. There is no point in trying to buy, or sell, a house, for more than it is worth by regarding the extra as 'Just a bit more on the mortgage', and therefore, simply an extra pound or so on the repayment.

Neither is there any point in trying to cover the cost of fittings, fixtures or carpets in the mortgage application, on the same basis. You will be found out and your credibility with the Building Society severely damaged.

There are other sources of mortgage money which may be worth investigating. The High Street banks offer mortgages, and many Estate Agents have now joined forces with insurance companies to do the same. Whatever you decide, make sure you know exactly what it will cost you. It may not be quite as straightforward as it first appears.

And now you know the worst and find yourself in one of three categories. Either you can raise an adequate mortgage; you are just a little short; or you have no hope, at present, of raising enough to be of any practical use.

The first group can skip the next chapter. Its purpose is to go further into the problems of the others, particularly the last.

Take heart. We are not beaten yet.

3

Alternatives to Buying

The man who finds that his mortgage offer is not quite enough to purchase the type of house which he wants, has a number of choices.

He can review his requirements and decide whether a more modest house would be adequate. On the other hand, he can decide to wait, save more deposit, and come back, when he can afford to pay more.

The problem with this last suggestion is that house prices have, in some years, increased at such a rate that it would take a man with a huge income to save fast enough, even to keep up with it. And such a person is unlikely to have mortgage problems, in the first place.

Of course, the rate of rise varies but, generally speaking, the brutal fact is that, even at the slowest rate experienced in the last twenty years, it is extremely unlikely that you will be able to save at anything like an adequate rate to keep pace.

You must seek a way of buying a house for less than it is worth. Impossible, you say? Not quite.

Over the past ten years, or so, growing concern at the worsening housing situation has led many people to try to find ways around the difficulties. For a number of reasons, two suggestions have proved to be more successful than most. They are Self-Build-Groups and Co-ownership Schemes.

Both receive help and guidance from the Housing Corporation, an official body whose aim is to stimulate this sort of housing effort.

Anyone can take on the job of building his own house. Many people have. Their success is very much dependent on their skill as handymen. They also meet a number of financial difficulties. The Self-Build-Group goes a long way to answering these.

The principle is a simple one. By combining their resources, a group of people can raise the money to buy a piece of land on which they will build houses for their own use. Often the Council will sell them the land; sometimes even lending them the money to do so. The group, usually with the help of a local Architect, or Surveyor, obtains Planning Permission, buys materials and sets about the job of 'do-it-yourself' house building.

Supervision and expert knowledge are often to be found in the average group, but, in order to avoid dispute, a proper management committee is formed, with a Chairman, Secretary and Treasurer.

Each member contributes his share of the costs of repaying loans, buying materials, etc, as the work proceeds. These are the only costs required. Labour is provided by the members of the group and costs nothing, unless it is felt that it is better to employ a tradesman to do a job which is beyond the members' skill.

A variation is to negotiate an arrangement with a Building Society, or the Council, to advance part of the costs, as the work proceeds, on a mortgage. This means that bigger schemes can be tackled on the Self-Build-Group basis.

When the first house is completed, the Group members usually draw lots to see who will have it. The lucky winner then takes possession, AS A TENANT, paying rent to the Group. The reason for this is that the Group must always be in a position to insist that each member still does his share of the work, even after he is re-housed.

By insisting on a tenancy, they reserve the right to discipline, even remove backsliders. This is fair enough. Everyone must pull his weight, right through the scheme, or the group will become unworkable.

When all the work is done, costs are added up and each person buys his house from the group. As labour costs are a substantial part of the price of a new house, the cost, to each group member is bound to be much less than buying on the open market.

A smaller price must mean a smaller mortgage.

If this idea interests you, ask the Surveyor, at the local Council Office, if there are any Self-Build-Groups being formed in the area. Failing that, write to the Housing Corporation. Their address is given in the Appendix of useful addresses, at the end of the book.

Co-Ownerships are rather different. You do not necessarily need to work on the house, yourself, and you do not actually become owner of your individual house.

What you will do is to buy shares in the Managing Company and become part-owner, with all the other tenants, of the houses which are rented to you and the others, by the company. Thus, you are a tenant, without the need to carry a private mortgage, but you will also exercise control over the scheme by being a Co-Owner with the right to vote at management meetings.

The scheme will be financed initially from the money advanced to buy the shares. Usually counted in hundreds of pounds, rather than the thousands required to buy a house, this is seldom beyond the savings of the average man. Repayments of the Company's mortgage for the rest of the money are made out of the rent charged to each tenant.

If you wish to move, you will have to sell your shares to the next tenant and this will mean that any increased value in the property will be reflected in what you get for them. It is fair to say, however, that you should not expect the same sort of capital profit that you would look for, on the sale of your own house. The method by which your share will be valued is set out in your tenancy agreement, and is explained, in general terms, in Appendix 3. The Sum which you may receive is known as a Premium Payment.

Co-Ownership is a method of combining the financial muscle power of several people, in order to give equal benefit to all, including those whose resources are limited.

If you would like to know more, write to the Housing Corporation about this type of scheme also.

Co-Ownerships may also decide to wind up the group and to sell the houses to the people who occupy them. Since the group is only required to clear its mortgage and any other debts, the tenant members often buy their houses for much less than their market value. Those who have been in occupation longest pay the least.

Ideally the decision to wind up would be unanimous. If it is not, those who wish to buy their property can form a company to buy the houses of those who wish to remain tenants but this is complicated and usually requires special compensation to those not buying. Legal advice is essential before following this course.

The only other alternative is to move to an area where the general level of prices is lower.

This is not meant as a funny crack. It may be an answer. Obviously it depends on several factors. Is there work in the lower priced area? Could you do that type of work, anyway? Are you and, more important, is your partner willing to leave your family contacts?

It is a big decision to make but it could be worth it. Television, films and modern opportunities to travel have, long ago, destroyed the old idea that a Devon man is a Foreigner in Yorkshire. You can put that worry right out of your head. If your parents try to persuade you to stay locally, the pressures on you will be unbearable. The only advice which we can give you is to say that it is your life and happiness that are at stake. You cannot live solely for other people and your parents cannot live your lives for you.

However, if you cannot see your way to following any of these alternatives, you must join the last of our three groups – those who cannot think in terms of buying a house, at least for some time yet.

The sad fact is that the problems of housing yourself in property which you have not bought are so daunting that few people have thought it worth the trouble of trying to help. The result is that house-seekers, in this field, have very little guidance available to them.

The rest of this chapter is an effort to meet this omission, for what it is worth.

By far the biggest landlords, in this country, are the various local Councils. You may not want a council house, or flat, but you must ask yourself, seriously, are you going to get anything better?

Of course, the long waiting lists, at almost every Council Office, are notorious and you will be very fortunate if you get a Council tenancy very quickly. For all that, it can do no harm to try. You lose nothing by calling at the Council Office and filling in a form.

Tenants of council housing now have a right to buy their houses at various discounts off the full value. Information about this right can be obtained from the Citizens Advice

Bureau. It is also obtainable from the Council Housing Department but not all councils approve of the plan, which has been forced on them by Central Government, and some do not go out of their way to help people who seek advice. In any case, discounts only become due after you have occupied the house for three years or more and that is small comfort to people who are not yet even tenants.

Keep in touch with the local Estate Agents. They seldom have anything to let, but, just occasionally – you never know.

What they may be offering is likely to be pretty awful and by no means cheap. Try not to get so desperate that you jump into any old thing.

You will find that, in most cases, internal decorations must be done by you. Be very careful, here. Think hard about the cost of decorating a really old building, and even harder before you do structural improvements. You will receive no compensation, or return of any kind, even if you leave the property looking like a palace. It is up to you, but, again, be warned.

See page 20 for more information about the renting of furnished property.

It is quite understandable that people, desperate for somewhere to live, should turn to caravans. Many newspapers contain glowing advertisements, offering this type of accommodation as the answer to every housing problem.

Caravans are cheaper than houses and can be very pleasant, with their crisp, clean interiors and their well planned layouts. When you decide to move, you will be told, you simply take your home with you. The life of a gypsy always seems romantic. It is not surprising that many people take up this means of housing themselves.

The first point to remember is that you may well buy a caravan on very favourable terms. Unfortunately, whatever may happen to house values, caravans are sure to go down in value, if only for the reason that they are not built to last as long.

Secondly, you will be very lucky, and almost unique, if you can buy a site for your caravan, at the same time. Normally you must rent one and the truth is that sites are by no means as easy to find as caravans to put on them.

Most Caravan Sites are holiday sites and do not want the bother of residential 'vans. Regrettably, not all site owners are honest and some caravan residents have discovered, too late, that no Planning Permission was ever obtained for the use of the site by Caravans.

In such circumstances, Planning Authorities are quite within their rights to require you to move and they are under no obligation to provide you with somewhere to move to.

If the salesman at the caravan dealer's tells you that he can find a site for you, ask him to let you have that statement in writing, as a condition of your purchase of a 'van; and watch him back-pedal.

Even if he does not do so, still be careful. Do not let him get away with promising to 'try' to find you a site. He could try to put you in orbit. He can even start to build a rocket, but he will almost certainly fail and you will have no real case to make against him.

Never agree to 'buy' a site, or pay more than the 'van is worth, on the grounds that the site goes with it. Unless, of course, the seller owns the site, or has a lease, and can show you the deeds to prove it.

If you 'rent' a site, you will find that, in certain circumstances, the owner will need the Court's consent to evict you and you will enjoy certain legal rights. In practice, these are rather less than those enjoyed by the tenant of a house. With such a limited hold on a site, no tenant has anything to sell and you are being very foolish if you fall for such a dirty trick. Unfortunately, there are always people who will try it on. If you come across such a one, take our advice and withdraw. You are getting yourself into very muddy waters.

And, speaking of muddy waters, that other popular substitute, the House Boat, is almost exactly the same. No security of tenure on a mooring, rents which can soar and the added risk of drowning.

Perhaps you feel that this is exaggerated. Well, perhaps it is, a little; but the warning still holds good. A modern house boat, on a mooring, can seem the ideal solution. Unfortunately, if the mooring is only going to be yours for the month, until the owner throws you off it, it is pretty useless to you.

The attractions of buying an old cottage, and doing it up,

over a year or so, will always appeal, particularly to the handyman.

You may feel that this provides another answer for the desperate home seeker but, you might just as well be disillusioned now, as later. The difficulties of getting mortgages on properties which need major repairs and the popularity of renovating, amongst people who can afford it, has, long ago, killed off any benefit there might have been for the less well off, in this area.

Have you considered the possibility of moving to a New Town. There are so many, now, that it is unlikely that you are very far from one. There are two types; New Towns, which are being built virtually from nothing, and Expanded Towns. These are being based on older towns, which provide a sense of already existing community.

Both are anxious to attract people to live in them. There are usually jobs, and modern, publicly owned houses for rent. Your chances of being allocated one are rather better than those of becoming a council tenant, in your own area.

Your local Housing Office will tell you where the nearest New Towns are, and, if they have no other information, you can always write. A letter, asking for information about employment opportunities, in the New Town, and also the possibilities of renting a house, will be quite adequate.

Address it to the Publicity Officer, Somewhere New Town Corporation, Somewhere, Somewhereshire. It may not be strictly correct, in every case, but it will almost certainly get to the right person.

Some industrialists, who have opened factories in a New Town, are allocated so many rented houses for the people who go to work for them. That might be your chance. In any case, it brings us to another possibility.

Some jobs include housing accommodation, as a condition of employment. Of course, if you are a tradesman, with specific skills and training, you may not be very keen on giving them up; but there is always the chap who turns his hand to whatever job happens to be available, and he may well wish to consider this suggestion.

The retail trade – shop management, for instance, has a tradition of, literally, living over the shop. This is particularly so in the Licensed Trade. Could you manage a 'pub, or a hotel?

No harm can come of your writing to the Secretary of your local brewery company. The address will be in the telephone directory.

The work of a 'landlord' – a strange and entirely inaccurate name – covers two different positions. You can manage a 'pub, being paid a salary, or you can take a tenancy. In this case, you rent the 'pub, usually fairly cheaply, and you buy the business. It therefore becomes your business, until you sell it to the next tenant, and your income is the profit which you make.

Obviously, the best return comes from being a tenant, but this will entail your having enough money to buy the business, in the first place. It may be more than you can afford anyway.

In practice, many people start as managers and then save up enough money to enable them to become tenants.

Not everyone is fitted for this exacting work. Think hard about it, before you commit yourself.

Farming is another industry with a tradition of providing housing for its labourers, but, again, a few words of warning.

The word, labourer, is a particularly unfortunate one, for the farm worker. He has suffered from its undertone of mindless muscle, for a very long time. The name is accurate, in so far as the work is hard, backbreaking and entails long hours. If it suggests that the work is unskilled, it is totally untrue. Farm workers are very skilled men, indeed, in a remarkable range of different ways.

Farming is not something which you can just turn round and do. However, it may be that you have some specific mechanical skill which would be of use, on a farm, and this may be your opportunity.

Of course, it would entail your living in the country and you must give that fact considerable thought. Most townspeople have only ever seen the countryside in good weather. It can be unbelievably dull, in the rain.

The whole question of living in the country is discussed in the next chapter. If you are considering taking a job there, you might find it useful to read the appropriate section.

For some reason, uniformed jobs have always tended to mean accommodation. You may feel that becoming a soldier, in order to get a house, is a rather dramatic thing to do, but there are other possibilities. The Police Force is tending to encourage men to buy their own houses, nowadays, but they still have a considerable number of houses which are let to policemen, as quarters. Much the same can be said of the Fire Service.

There are excellent opportunities for promotion, in either service, although certain standards of fitness must be met and long, often inconvenient hours must be worked.

Prison Officers are also housed in quarters and the Prison Service does offer the chance of a worthwhile career. You are probably not aware that many Prison Officers are instructors, so that your trade need not be wasted. You can teach and supervise men serving their sentences, in useful work. There is satisfaction in helping a man to make a new start.

People forget that Prisons are large buildings and that someone has to maintain and repair them. This work is supervised by building tradesmen, who are also Prison Officers. They too, have quarters. If you are in the building trade, this could be an answer, for you.

The great problem with 'tied' houses – that is, houses which come with the job – is that they GO with the job, as well. If you resign, you lose the house. Worse, if you die, or are injured, and cannot carry on with your job, you, or your wife and family may be required to move out. The same applies when you retire.

For this reason, you should never get complacent. Always regard the tied property as a temporary measure, and look out for something more secure, all the time. If you leave it too late, you will find that you have no time left to save a deposit and that you must either take a short term, expensive mortgage, or run the repayment period into your retirement. Very few Building Societies are keen on that.

Obviously, it would be the poorest reason, if you selected your future career, simply because a house went with it; but there is an old saying:

'Never marry for money. Marry where money is.' This advice also applies where tied houses are concerned. Never choose your career because it brings housing accommodation, but let it be a point to bear in mind.

4

What Do We Choose?

The degree of choice open to the home seeker depends on the length of his purse. If he only has, or can only borrow, the amount required to buy the cheapest house available, then his choice is obviously very limited.

On the other hand, there is the person to whom money is no object and his degree of choice goes well beyond what anyone else would look for.

The great majority of us come somewhere between these two extremes and, for the purposes of this chapter, let us assume that you are not too badly placed, financially, and can look round for a wider range of possibilities.

If you open your paper, they will all be there. Dozens, sometimes hundreds of them. All set out, some with photographs, all with their neat price tag; at least, almost all. Those which have no price are usually on sale at a figure which even the Estate Agent is frightened to mention.

The mention of prices raises the first point for you to remember.

The house market is almost the last place of business, in Britain, where you are expected to bargain and haggle. Few people expect to get the price which they ask for their houses and most put a little on the price, in order to give themselves room for manoeuvre.

This means that you need never restrict your search to properties priced at, or below, your top limit. Always feel free to look at houses priced at a few hundred or a thousand or two pounds more.

The real strain comes when you have set yourself a limit of so many thousand pounds. Every Estate Agent has met the man who refused to look at a house priced at £50,100, because it was over his limit of £50,000. The mistake, of course, was putting such a silly price on, in the first place, but he was almost as short sighted. The house might well have suited him, and few vendors would have stuck out for a hundred pounds.

There is one notable exception to this general rule. Builders of new properties set a price and often have several identical houses to sell, at that price. They will seldom be open to negotiation and the reason is fairly obvious.

If you had bought a house, on an estate, and then discovered that your neighbours, who had bought after you, had paid less than you, for an identical house; you would be displeased, to say the least. In practice, there would be little you could do about it, but most builders can do without the nasty remarks that you are certain to make to your friends and his future customers.

Builders do, occasionally, reduce prices, but the reasons are usually based on overall market conditions, not pressure from one possible purchaser.

But, back to our newspaper. You will see, at once, that it is never as simple as just deciding on one house, out of many. You must first decide, where you want to live, town or country; what you wish to live in, house or bungalow, or flat; how many bedrooms; do you need a garage; old property or new, etc. etc.

Before your head really begins to spin, let us try to get some order into this.

There are really only a few basic considerations, in deciding just what will meet your needs. These tend to throw up subsidiary questions, but we can deal with them as they arise.

First of all, where do you want to live? The first part of that answer must be, distance from work, shops and schools.

'Nearness' is a word which means different things to different people. To a Londoner, thirty miles from his office is 'near'. Many travel sixty miles to work, some even further. The secret is, of course, that the transport facilities, in London, are so good. We all complain about them, but they still manage to deliver several hundred thousand people to work, each morning, and take them home at night.

Smaller towns seldom entail your travelling so far, but they generally have poorer transport facilities. And, of course, a journey of ten miles can be a very long one, if it

crosses a major road intersection, just when everyone else is
trying to get across as well.

And what about shopping facilities? Are there some shops
within easy walking distance? If not, will you always have
transport to reach them? Is there a convenient regular bus
service?

The children have got to get to school. There is a great
deal to be said for them living within walking distance.

Another point that many people forget, is that transport,
be it public or in your own car, is not free. On the contrary,
costs go up all the time. Are the advantages of that remote
cottage so great that you can afford an extra five, perhaps
ten pounds, each week for travelling? Even worse, is the
smaller mortgage which you required because the house was
remote and cheaper, really a bargain, if your transport costs
use up all the savings you made?

Which brings us to the other aspect of the same problem –
whether you wish to live in the country or in the town; and
here, we are on very uncertain ground. Perhaps we had
better decide just what we mean by the words, first.

There is a story of a couple who had always wished to live
in the country and bought a house in Croydon. They were
happy all their lives because they considered that they had
achieved their ambition. A very eminent scientist used to tell
his friends that, whenever the pressures of the city got too
much for him, he would take a bus to Shepherd's Bush and
get some country air.

It is all relative. To the person from Stepney, or Tooting
or Brixton; if the houses are a few feet apart, that is the
countryside. To the man from Winterbourne Bishop, or
Much Wenchin-in-the-Wood; anywhere where they can see
more than five houses, at one time, is the town; and if it has
two shops, that settles it.

There would be no problem if people would only decide
what kind of area they want and go and live there. If it
makes them happy to think of it as something that it is not,
no one is hurt, so let them do so. Unfortunately, people will
confuse the real countryside with what is really suburbia.
They assume that a childhood in the rural delights of
Putney, qualifies them to live somewhere like Bumble
Hole, or Midden Magna.

We are told that, in every townsman, is a countryman, trying to get out. All too often, when he actually tries living in the country, he is soon trying, desperately, to get back in again.

A cess-pit may seem terribly amusing; until there is three feet of snow; the 'Lavender Waggon' cannot come to empty it, and the contents meet you, coming down the garden path. Oil lamps do give a lovely, soft light. They can also give fumes, a nasty smell and leave stains on the wallpaper.

No, it is far wiser to accept that, unless you are a very special type of person, preferably used to country life, you are far better advised to forget it.

It seems that the dream of so many people, is to find a derelict, old cottage, renovate it and live happily, ever after. In practice, a great many people have done just that. So could you. Providing, of course, you do not see it as a means of getting a house cheaply. The very popularity of the idea has finished that possibility. On the other hand, if you have the money and are prepared for many more problems than you ever expect, you can find it a very rewarding exercise.

However, if, after a while, you find that country living is rather a burden, you will find yourself with a half renovated property on your hands and which you cannot sell easily. Your ideas of modernization and renovation are most unlikely to coincide with anyone else's and you may find it difficult to get back the money which you have already spent.

Renovation is a very complicated subject and cannot be dealt with fully, here. For the moment, accept that there are attendant problems and think hard about the whole idea of living in rural bliss.

In the end, most of us finish up in an environment which we find comfortable, pleasant and convenient. When we move, we simply go to another area, of the same type. It is usually quite near to those shops which you require regularly and within a short ride of the bigger shops, which we all need, occasionally. All this and yet the countryside is usually within a mile or so.

Remarkably, this idyllic place has the most unpleasant

image and is more subjected to sneers than anywhere else. It is called Suburbia.

Quite why the Trendy and Superior are so unkind about Suburbia, is a mystery. Perhaps they are ashamed of their origins. That is their business. In fact, the great majority of us live there, and seldom find it to be the unbearable place which we are apparently supposed to.

The chances are that you will find the same, if you would only give it a try. Do not allow the comments of your so-called friends, or the prejudices which you will have accumulated, over the years, to put you off. The odds are that you will find what you are seeking, in a suburban area. Accept the fact, and your search will be quicker and easier.

And now, let us consider the accommodation which you will need. The more floor space you require, the more the house will cost, and it is very tempting to buy a house with two bedrooms, because it is cheaper than one with three. This can be false economy. Two bedroom bungalows are really built for couples whose children have grown up and left home. And, even they find it rather overcrowded, when all the family comes to stay, at the same time.

Time and time again, one sees younger couples moving into a small property, only to move out again, within a year or so, because they now have a family and need more space.

The value of a third bedroom is particularly obvious when you have bought a house, some distance from your home area. Your parents will want to visit you and this may mean staying overnight. There is nothing much less pleasant than giving up your bed and camping on the settee; unless it is expecting your parents to sleep there. Do consider this aspect, when you work out your actual needs.

On the other hand, do not over-estimate them, either. This is more likely to happen when you consider the size of the garden.

We all like privacy and a large garden does tend to provide it. It only does so at a price. You are forced to look after it, to dig it, weed it and mow it. How keen are you on this sort of exercise?

It could well be that that impressive garden will take up

most of your free time and a large slice out of your spare cash. If you are an enthusiast, that will be marvellous. If you are not, it will be the most burdensome responsibility you can take on.

Do you need a garage? There can only be one answer to that question. You may not own a car; you may never intend to have one. It makes no difference. Always aim for a house with a garage; or, at least, garage space, if at all possible.

Statistics show that more and more people are becoming car owners. As time goes by, a house which has no garage, or space, will be attractive to fewer and fewer people. The dangers to you, when you come to sell the house, are obvious.

We live in a status-conscious age and it is disturbing to see how many people are giving themselves worry and hard work, because of it. They cannot bring themselves to buy something which they can afford but which is not up to the standards which they have set themselves.

Ask yourself, seriously, is it essential for you to have a detached house? For that matter, is it essential that you have a semi-detached house? Terrace houses provide homes for millions of families, up and down the country.

There is something to be said for being kept warm by the fire in your neighbour's grate.

More important, why take on a maximum mortgage, when you can buy a more modest house, at a lower price, and which will meet your needs.

This is particularly the case with older property. Being old does not necessarily mean being sub-standard. Many Victorian houses were built to very high standards and provide solid, spacious homes. You may well find that you can buy a house with better accommodation, for a lower cost, if you are prepared to accept such a house.

If there are any services which are not laid on, then this is an excellent reason for getting the price reduced. You can always have them connected, in due course.

Of course, there is a limit to all this, and you will usually find that it is set by the Building Society. They have no need to lend money to buy ancient monuments. There are always plenty of people seeking loans to buy nice, safe, reliable modern houses. Inevitably, most Societies draw a line which makes it clear just what older houses they will accept and which they will decline.

Even when you can raise money to buy something which was built as a house, however old it may be; you will almost certainly find difficulty in financing the purchase of something which was never meant to be a house, in the first place.

Oast houses, windmills, light houses; they have all been converted, by someone, at some time. But please believe that this is a field for people who are just a shade eccentric and who have no real money problems. Alteration work, of this sort, is difficult and continually turns up more problems, as it proceeds. You need time and a very long purse, if you are going to bring it to a satisfactory conclusion.

To sum up, try to remember a few rules.

Do not set your standards too high. Even if you can afford them, you are silly to take on a mortgage which is higher than it need be.

Do not make dramatic moves into surroundings which are not those to which you are used. If you have always enjoyed certain services; 'bus, electricity, shops, etc., you cannot visualize what life is like without them.

Do not turn your nose up at older property.

Consider, very carefully, if you are skilled enough to take on the renovation work that a derelict house will need.

Remember, Suburbia is the entirely acceptable home of most of us. Only the Trendies look down on it, and they are so fickle that, next year, they are just as likely to be in favour of it.

This chapter has tried to put the facts before you and to help you get your own thoughts in some order. That is all it can do. In the end, you must decide.

5

How to Organize Your Search

You are now ready to move a step forward. You have
worked out what you can afford and what sort of house you
would like. Now you can start to look for it.

If you are searching in your home area, then the next step
is quite straightforward. If, on the other hand, you are
moving to another part of the country, then you have a little
spade work to do, first.

The bigger the town where you propose to live, the
better the transport facilities are likely to be, and the more
of a problem you will face. Just where are you going to
live?

There are a number of aspects to this problem. Firstly,
some areas, just as convenient to the main centre, tend to
have a cheaper property market. When you go there, you
can usually see why, but that does not always rule them out.
You can check this aspect by buying a copy of one of the
magazines which cater for the home seeker. They are to be
found on most bookstall magazine racks.

Each edition usually contains details of properties on
offer, in various counties. A few minutes with a map will
show you which counties you are interested in, and, by comparing properties with similar accommodation, and, if there
is a photograph, appearance, you will soon work out the
comparisons.

Spend a day or so, just driving, or walking, round the
areas and getting the feel of them. You will soon begin to
receive impressions – those subconscious vibrations by
which you know that you 'like this place' but could never
live in that place. By then, your mind will have been made
up, and, after checking train times and fares, just to be sure,
you can start looking.

There are three obvious sources of information for you.
The newspapers, the Estate Agents and the notices on the

houses, themselves. These will overlap, in practice, but that does not matter.

During your preliminary trips, you will almost certainly have noticed sale boards, and possibly, you may already have contacted the Estate Agent for more information. By far the great majority of boards and adverts in the paper will refer you back to one or another Estate Agent and, as a result, he makes an excellent place to start.

An agent is a person who is legally empowered to enter into contracts, on behalf of another person – usually called the Principal. On these terms, an Estate Agent is not really an agent at all. He very seldom has legal power to commit his client to anything; on the contrary, he must almost always, obtain the agreement of his Principal, before agreeing to accept any offer that you make.

In modern terms, he is really a Broker; a man who introduces a buyer to a seller. The word agent dates from the time when almost every land owner was a wealthy man, spending most of his time away from his estates. He needed someone to arrange things while he was absent and the profession of land agency was born.

This does not mean that Estate Agents do not offer a useful service; if only by providing a central office where details of houses may be obtained. It does mean that their role, and loyalties, are likely to be rather confused.

When you ask an Estate Agent for details of a house which is on his books, you are simply seeking information. You have no obligation to buy and he has no duty to you, apart from the standards of honesty and fair dealing, imposed by law.

His duty is to the man who will be paying his fee; the Seller of the house.

He will be polite and helpful to the buyer, but his job is to persuade you to buy his client's house, not to tell you that it might not be what you are looking for.

If he is able to arrange a mortgage for you, his aim is to ease the sale along, in the interests of the seller; not necessarily to tell you that another Society might give you more advantageous terms.

Now, please believe that he is not going to rob you or take evil advantage of you. In fact, the great majority of Agents take their position very seriously and try to be fair to everyone. In the end, however, their interests cannot be your interests. You must guard these for yourself.

You will have no difficulty in making contact with the Agent. As you enter his office, you will be greeted immediately and politely asked what you are looking for. The Estate Agent's Negotiator – as he is called – will probably check that you really know your financial position. No harm in that, but you can always tell him that you have confirmed the position with the XYZ Building Society. He will accept that.

He will show you the details of a whole range of properties; many of them, not really what you are looking for, at all. That does not matter. Far better turn them down than risk missing the right one.

The printed details which he will give you are called 'particulars'. Over the years, a whole language has grown up, solely for use in Agent's particulars. It is flowery, ornate and, providing you read it carefully, and discount the adjectives, it can be very accurate and helpful.

Since the passing of the Trades Descriptions Act, any trader trying to sell something has had to be very careful as to what they say about it. Estate Agents have, by now, become very competent at going as far as they dare. For instance, it is quite acceptable to say 'delightfully situated'. That is an expression of his opinion. You may not agree, but he might like the idea of living next to the gasworks. If, on the other hand, he says that the house has five bedrooms when, in fact, it only has two, that is a mis-statement of fact and is an offence. This has made Estate Agents, and others, for that matter, rather more careful.

Basically, all that you need to know about a house is; how many bedrooms it has; an indication of their size; whether the house has a garage; whether there is a garden and whether it is at the back or the front of the house; whether it is semi-detached, detached or terraced.

If you look for that information, and ignore the verbiage, you can be reasonably certain that what you read is accurate. There are, however, a few small points to watch.

Almost any room, situated on the first floor, tends to be described as a bedroom. Check the sizes given and see if the room will take a bed and a chest-of-drawers. If no sizes are given, you can assume that the Estate Agent felt that they were too awful to risk including.

This goes for any room, where dimensions have been missed out, with one exception – the bathroom. If it has a bath, a wash basin and a W.C, it is sure to be big enough. After all, you only need room to stand and work a towel backwards and forwards.

Beware also, of rooms described by a square foot measurement. Here too the Agent must have a reason for being deliberately confusing. You can assume that the room is of a very peculiar shape.

You may see the letters I.B. after one of the room measurements. This stands for 'into bay', and means that the Agent measured the distance into the bay window. It may be a very large bay window, but, equally, it may not be. For the moment, deduct two feet from the dimension, in order to get a fair impression.

Another thing to watch out for is the use of dimensions described as 'maximum'. This means that the room is L-shaped, in which case the measurement is totally misleading. It could also mean that the room has a bay, an alcove or a chimney breast. All these things can give a misleading impression of the room itself.

If you suspect that one of these little traps is being set, ask the Negotiator to explain. You will be able to judge the truth of the matter by his reaction.

The price of the property normally will either be given at the front of the particulars or at the end.

If the property has been allowed to get into a state of disrepair (for example, if the roof, gutters or outside decoration is in a bad condition), then the price should reflect that fact.

Normally the asking price will be the value of the property, in good repair, less the cost of putting it back into that condition.

It follows, therefore, that if you see two houses for sale which are near to each other in the same part of town and which have the same number of rooms of approximately the same size and similar-sized gardens, but one is priced lower than the other, it is reasonable to assume that the cheaper property will require some additional expenditure on repair.

Also, at the end or front of the property's particulars immediately after the price you may notice the word Freehold or, sometimes (often if it's a flat), Leasehold. This calls for some explanation.

If you buy a freehold house, you buy it absolutely, without any reservations, and you become the owner. No one else has any form of interest in it, except the Queen, who, in theory, still owns all land in Britain. For all practical purposes, a Freeholder owns his property completely.

When a property is sold as a leasehold, the arrangement is rather more complicated. In effect, the owner allows you to occupy the ground for an agreed period, more often than not for ninety-nine years. This is called a Lease. In return, you pay so much a year, while you occupy. This is called the Ground Rent.

You may decide to build a house on a leasehold site, but, if you do, you only own it as long as the lease lasts. You can sell your lease to someone else, if you wish, but what you are really doing is selling the house and letting the purchaser take over the lease and the responsibility for paying the ground rent.

Obviously, a leasehold house should cost less than a freehold because you will only have it for a definite period and not for ever, although this last point is no longer strictly the case. Under existing law, it may be that you will be able to insist on buying the freehold, in due course. Of course, even if you do, this is no reason to pay more at the time you buy the leasehold. Otherwise you will be paying twice.

If you do not buy the freehold, at the end of the lease, you may well be able to demand the right to remain in the house as a protected, rent paying tenant.

Such an arrangement is perfectly fair, providing you know the limitations and pay a price which takes them into account. Unfortunately, some builders have seized on leasehold as a way of having things both ways. They can obtain a ground rent but also sell the house. All too often the price they ask is only a little less than the freehold price.

In practice, if the Building Society is happy with the price being asked, then you need not worry too much. If, however, you are asking for a fairly small mortgage, then it is not a bad idea to compare the cost of the leasehold houses with others which are similar but on offer as freeholds. As a rough guide, multiply the ground rent by ten and add the result to the leasehold price. If it is about the same as the equivalent freehold, then the arrangement is not too unfair. If it is much more, then the builder is being greedy.

There is a growing tendency to include photographs of houses in particulars. Growing because the customer expects it. Actually, few Estate Agents like photos. They can be very misleading.

All but a few houses seem to come into one of two brackets. There are attractive houses, which for some reason or another, cannot be photographed to their advantage, and ruinous old derelicts, which photograph very well. In such circumstances, the Agent cannot win. He either offends purchasers by sending them to look at totally unsuitable property, or vendors, because they find that people have been put off by the picture and never bothered to inspect.

You are best advised to ignore photographs, whether they encourage or discourage interest. Form your impression by analysing the wording of the particulars.

By looking at the particulars, with a clear head and a balanced eye, neither disbelieving or believing anything, without thinking about it, you will be able to evaluate the house pretty accurately.

The Estate Agent may offer to take you round the houses and this can be a great convenience to you. It puts you under no obligation but helps you to get round very much quicker. He knows where the houses are. You will have to find them.

Of the houses which he has to sell, some will be vacant and he will have a key; some will be occupied. If a vacant house is furnished, he will want to come with you. Do not be offended. He does not know you from Adam. In any case, he is protecting you. If anything was stolen and you had been allowed to inspect, on your own, who would be the main suspect? Empty houses can be inspected simply by borrowing the key, although, in these days of squatters, Agents are, quite sensibly, less inclined to let keys out so casually as in years gone by.

Occupied houses may be viewed, simply by calling; or,

perhaps, by making an appointment. The latter is becoming much more the accepted thing, although, few people will refuse to let you view on the off chance, if you have a good reason. For instance, you may only be in town for that afternoon. It is all a matter of give and take.

Just how you tackle the inspection of a property, and what you look for, is explained in the next chapter, but, before we leave this one, just a few further words about the Estate Agent.

He will require your name and address and will add your name to his list of applicants. If you refuse to tell him, he is quite entitled to refuse to give you any information at all. He is quite right to wish to know just who he is encouraging to call on his clients.

Some people seem to fear 'going on the list'. They complain of being 'bombarded by particulars'. If they are genuinely seeking a new house, this surely, is a good thing. It is the work of a few seconds to dismiss an obviously unsuitable house from your list, and far better that you eliminate them than the Agent fail to send them to you.

Estate Agents have all seen, too many times, the person who insists that he wants a detached house, and who then buys a semi. The person who must have four bedrooms, and finishes up buying a bungalow, with two. Added to that, the majority of people have difficulty with words. They describe to the Agent what they want and end up with so clear a picture in their own minds, that they imagine that the Agent has exactly the same picture in his.

In fact, the Agent will probably have obtained only the vaguest idea, from your comments. He soon learns that, by probing further, he risks offending you, and he simply takes the line of least resistance.

Do not imagine that he is trying to persuade you to buy something different from your first intentions. The chances are that he knows that you will do just that, anyway.

After your discussion, or having taken you to see all the houses which you wish to see, the Agent will bid you a polite good-bye; possibly even drive you back to the station. He will almost certainly have been kind, considerate and helpful to a fault. You will inevitably feel a sense of obligation to him.

And this is exactly what he wants. He may deny it. He may not even believe it, himself. It makes no difference. All the help, all the consideration is really an attempt to establish a sense of association, with him as 'your' Agent. He cannot be this in the legal sense, of course. He is aiming to create a sense of moral obligation, instead.

What you must be careful to avoid is any sense of obligation to buy a house which he is selling. There is no such obligation. The Agent provides a service. It is in his interests, and those of his client, the vendor, that he be polite and helpful to possible purchasers. On top of which, he knows that you might be a vendor yourself, some day.

He will not think any the worse of you, therefore, if you finally buy from one of his business rivals.

6

Building Surveys and 'Just Looking'

When you visit a house, with a view to buying it, you are really looking at it in two ways. You will be seeking a place in which you feel comfortable and can build a home: You will also be looking at a piece of building construction, into which you propose to sink a great deal of money.

As far as it is possible, you should aim to keep these two aspects separate, in your mind. Obviously, there is a limit to how far you can do this, but it must be your aim. There is great danger in so falling in love with a house that you ignore serious structural faults.

It is by far the best approach, if you look at the house as a future home, first, and then, when you are satisfied that it will suit you, look at in more detail. You can even benefit by making two separate visits. This does enable you to get the stars out of your eyes and make a second and detailed inspection with a head cleared of romantic first impressions.

You have already read that no one can sell you a 'home', but that you have to make it for yourself. It is equally true to say that no one can tell you if a house will make a 'home' which will suit you. Only you will know that and your decision will be almost instinctive.

All we can offer, here, is the most general advice, in the hope that it will help you to get your thoughts into some sort of order.

A home is where you feel comfortable and nothing destroys that feeling more quickly than inconvenience; lavatories placed miles away from bedrooms; steps between rooms supposedly on the same floor; awkward, twisted staircases.

Obviously, a disabled person will wish to avoid such

things, at all cost, but even a fit, healthy one will find them pretty annoying, once the quaintness has worn off.

Try to gauge just how your furniture will fit into each of the rooms, even if it is only your mind's eye. If you find this to be difficult, and many people do, compare the measurements with those in your present house. If you have not got one, compare them with your parents' house, or that of a friend. If you can get your furniture into a room twelve feet by ten feet, you will be certain to get it into one, fourteen by eleven.

This may seem a pernickety detail, but a few months spent living in a house which entails a cross between a route march and a mountaineering expedition, in order to leave the room, will soon convince you.

First of all, just what will you be buying, if you agree to take the house? There is a great deal of misunderstanding as to what fixtures and fittings actually go with the house, in a normal transaction. In fact, the Law is not always clear, but common sense is a pretty good guide.

Generally speaking, 'fixtures' are regarded as part of the freehold of the house. They include, by custom, television aerials, permanent buildings, lawns, etc., which should be left with the property. Lamp shades, light bulbs, and the like, can be removed, but not the Rose from which the light fitting hangs.

The real problem, and one which causes most unpleasantness, is that grey area where it is not strictly illegal to remove an item but where it shows a degree of bad faith if you do. Plug tops are the most common items to come under this heading.

Of the items which, beyond question, are not part of the freehold; you may find that the Vendor will either wish to include some of them in the price or will be willing to sell them to you, separately.

It is a good idea to ask the Vendor, at this point, just what he is including and the price of any items which you want, and to decide whether *you* want the items he is insisting that you have. Whether you take them or not is part of the general decision whether you buy that house.

If you feel that the Vendor is proposing to remove something which you regard as part of the house, ask your Solicitor for advice.

None of these points are enough to put you off a house, on their own. They are simply points to bear in mind, when you are making your decision that the house will suit you. Having made that decision, you must now consider the house itself.

The simplest way to check the structural state of a house is to pay a surveyor. Where older houses are concerned, this may well be the wisest course, in any case. Houses built within the last ten years will, in by far the majority of cases have a certificate issued by the National House Building Council. If the house is actually in course of erection when you buy it, a certificate will almost certainly be required by the Building Society, before they will lend a penny.

The Council – usually referred to as the NHBC – is an official body which inspects the houses being built by firms on its register, and issues a certificate of guarantee. This acts as an insurance which provides that any structural faults which appear, within ten years of building will be put right, either by the builder or the Council itself. This is a valuable protection, but when you are told that a certificate exists, try to check when it expires.

You should also bear in mind that there are defects for which the builder cannot be blamed. These are excluded from the guarantee. If you want to find out, in detail, just what is covered, send to the NHBC and ask for their literature. Their address is in the Appendix.

On the basis that older – that is pre 1914 – houses are probably best surveyed professionally and that houses, not yet ten years old, should have NHBC protection, the appointment of a Surveyor is really only in doubt where houses, built after 1918 and more than ten years ago, are concerned.

The chances are that that is exactly the sort of house which you are considering.

Obviously, the easiest way out is to appoint a surveyor, but it may not be the most practical. Let us take the decision a step at a time.

As explained earlier, it is now possible for a purchaser to see the Building Society surveyor's report. If this reveals problems but the Society is still prepared to lend, only you can decide whether to buy or not. If you decide not to buy, do not expect your survey fee back. The surveyor has done his work and is entitled to be paid.

If you are still in doubt, and the Building Society survey is not sufficiently detailed to help you, you may decide to have your own survey carried out.

If you decide to appoint a Surveyor, go to one who describes himself as a Chartered Surveyor or who has the letters FRICS or ARICS, after his name. Failing that, go to one who has the letters ASVA or FSVA.

The reason for this is that any one of them has had to satisfy a very selective examination board that he is sufficiently experienced to undertake the work.

Avoiding the offices of the Agent/Surveyor who is selling the house, you should call on a Surveyor and ask to see someone who could do a building survey for you. When you see him, explain the situation, and ask what his fee will be. It may well be a shock to you. There is always far more work involved than you imagine, and surveyors are as entitled to be paid a proper rate as anyone else.

If the fee is too much for you, or if you feel that you can do the job for yourself, then the whole question is opened up again.

Many people ask a builder to look over the house, for them. This can work but has one inherent danger. The Surveyor is trained to evaluate the degree of repair needed in a house. He will usually differentiate between repairs which require immediate attention and those which are not really serious enough to bother about.

Builders are trained to build and repair houses. Ask one to go over your house and his instinct will be to point out all necessary repairs. He seldom differentiates. He will simply list what he thinks needs doing.

The result is that a builder's report may well be enough to put you off the house entirely, when, in fact, there is not a great deal wrong with it.

There is a middle course. Look at the house, yourself, after reading the remainder of this chapter and, if you find something which concerns you, then decide whether to appoint a Surveyor.

It is no exaggeration to say that by far the majority of structural problems, in houses, arise from the penetration of damp, in one way or another. This is all the more strange, when one remembers that houses are made of porous materials and are always damp, to a degree.

What we are really saying is that problems arise when the dampness in the fabric of a house passes an acceptable level.

This is not the point when the water comes cascading down the walls. It is much earlier than that and much less easy to spot. You have to look for clues, rather than the wetness, itself.

Water comes into a house in several ways: Downwards, when it finds a faulty roof; upwards, when it finds a faulty damp proof course; sideways, when the wind blows it and, never forget, through pipes, because you want it to.

The least frequent is sideways penetration, mainly because water seldom comes one way for long periods, so the water never builds up in such quantities as to cause trouble.

In any case, modern houses are built in a way which prevents such penetration. If you examine a house under construction, you are almost certain to find that the outside walls actually consist of two walls, roughly two inches apart and pinned together with iron straps or wires. The gap is called a cavity, hence – Cavity Walls.

Apart from providing an insulation barrier, to help keep you warm, it ensures that any water which penetrates as far as the cavity cannot go beyond it. The straps, or ties, being metal, will not convey the water over. Some careless bricklayers will sometimes allow mortar to build up on the ties and this will convey water, destroying the value of the cavity. It is something which you can watch out for, if you are buying a new house, and get the foreman to put a stop to it.

Water coming downwards can mean a faulty roof, but it is more likely to indicate blocked, or broken gutters. A straightforward, sloping roof is unlikely to cause trouble. The problems usually arise with older, more complicated roofs with hips and valleys. These used to be covered, or 'flashed' with lead, and, over the years, it may have worn away. Lead is rather expensive, nowadays, and the tendency has been to use felt for repairs. This is never as satisfactory as lead. If the house has any hips, valleys or bends, treat it with suspicion.

Evidence of downward dampness is usually found as patches on the ceilings and upstairs walls, working down from the ceilings. If there is only one patch, it is probably not too serious. You will usually find out what is wrong by climbing a ladder and taking a look. The repairs involved will probably be fairly limited.

Where there are stains, all around a house, then you have a more serious situation. Possibly, the answer will be to strip the roof and start again, but this need not put you off the house. Ask a builder for a price to do the work and make your offer to the owner, less the cost of the repairs.

Rising dampness is more serious still, because it suggests that there is damage to the Damp Proof Course. As the ground, in Britain, anyway, is always damp, to some degree, the brickwork in the foundations of a house will soak it up.

Left to itself, it would soon spread through the whole house and so, in all modern and most older houses, three or four brick courses above the ground, and below floor level, the builder will lay a Damp Proof Course – water tight skin of some sort. He then builds the rest of the house on top of it. Nowadays, it is usually a mineral felt, or plastic sheet. These are flexible and will bend to allow for any movement in the house. The old system was to use slate and this does not bend. A slight settlement of the brickwork will break the slate and allow water to pass up the crack and through the house.

If you are viewing an older house, with a damp stain centred on a point near the skirting board, you can assume that the Damp Proof Course is failing in its duty. It may be no more serious than a pile of dirt, against the wall, which has risen higher than the course and is acting as a bridge. In such a case, you simply remove the dirt. On the other hand, if the DPC itself is damaged, what can be done?

You can get a builder to go round the house, knocking bricks out, as he goes, and inserting a DPC instead. It is a long, expensive procedure and by no means guaranteed.

You can call in one of the firms who specialize in patent systems. They advertise widely and will usually give you a free estimate of the cost of what needs doing. They also offer a guarantee, but this can only be a cash guarantee, if all else fails. It is not much comfort when you find yourself forced to live in a damp house. However, these systems do have a good success rate.

A really badly affected house, with rising damp everywhere, is best left alone. In the end, the only answer is to take the house down to the foundations and start again. Hardly a practical suggestion.

The dampness which arises from burst pipes is usually dealt with fairly easily. If the pipes are laid beneath the floor boards, it is no problem to lift them and find the burst. Pipes which are laid in concrete entail chipping it away until you find them. In practice, this is far easier than making the surface good and as neat as before, when the pipe is mended.

There remains that last dampness which, for want of a better name, we call 'ghost dampness'. This usually appears as patches on the wall and defies any attempt to cure it, or even to locate the cause. You can paper over it with a sheet of proprietry water proof material, if you wish, but it always seems to appear somewhere else. Fortunately, it is seldom so serious that you cannot live with it.

Dampness of any sort has two secondary effects which can be very serious, indeed. These are Wet Rot and, illogically, Dry Rot. They are both defects found in the timber of the house.

Wet Rot occurs when the wood becomes so saturated that the fibres break apart, weakening the wood. It tends to happen at the ends of the timbers, where water can get in between the fibres, but it can occur elsewhere.

Depending upon how far the rot has gone, it can be cured by taking out the affected timber and replacing it with new. You can even cut off the end of an affected beam and fasten on another end, with bolts and side plates.

Dry Rot is much more insidious. It is a fungus which likes to live in damp conditions but breaks up the timber in a different way. It also gets down between the fibres but, instead of wetting them apart, it dries them. Dry Rotted timber looks almost as though it has been kiln dried to a brown, cracked appearance. It crumbles to dust, at a touch.

If a Dry Rot infestation were as easy to spot as that, it would not be too much of a problem. Unfortunately, the damage has been done long before any visible evidence appears. If you want to avoid the problem, you must look for the conditions in which Dry Rot thrives. These are damp, smelly, unventilated corners.

If the house has wooden floors, make sure that there are air bricks, built into the outside wall, below floor level. Push a stick through each one and check that it goes right through the wall and is not blocked in any way. Raise a floor board and sniff. You will know if it is well ventilated quickly enough. If it is not, then the danger signals are there.

If the house has a cellar, the chances are that the floor joists are exposed. Take a good, powerful torch and look along the timbers for any signs of Wet or Dry Rot. The two are quite different. Wet Rot breaks down the wood into soggy, separate fibres, when you rub it between your fingers. Dry Rot shows the typical cracking into square sections and breaks down into powder when you touch it.

Because of the probable spread to apparently sound timber, Dry Rot may well entail tearing out almost all the timber in the room – possibly even in the house. A house which is clearly affected is best left to someone who can afford to do the very expensive repairs.

Another problem which you may find in the timbers of the house is beetle, or woodworm. The different types of beetle can be dealt with together. Woodworm is the caterpillar of the beetle. The worms eat timber, working their way through it, and making tunnels, as they go. They usually take care to keep below the surface and a piece of wood may be eaten, and seriously weakened, without you being able to see any evidence of it.

The familiar 'flight' holes are caused when the worm completes its metamorphosis into a beetle. She digs her way out and either injects her eggs into the same piece of timber or flies away and finds another piece for the same purpose.

Whether any worms, or eggs remain is always difficult to say and the only way to be safe is to fill up the holes with one of the insecticides which the ironmonger will have in stock.

This will still leave one problem. Is the timber affected so badly as to be dangerous? This can be tested by pushing a thin knife blade, or a skewer, into the various timbers. If it goes in too easily, suspect the worst.

Badly worm eaten timber can be replaced and your decision must be based on the amount of repair required.

With any timber fault, you will need to lift a few floor boards, preferably those nearest to the skirting board, on the outside wall. You are also advised to climb into the roof space and look at the timber there. If the owner refuses to let you do so, again, assume the worst and let the house go.

We mentioned earlier, Page 56, the possibility of settlement and, in case you took fright at such a suggestion, set your minds at rest. All houses settle, to some extent. In new houses this can often be seen as cracking on the plaster. You would normally wait for six months, or so, and then simply fill the cracks with plaster.

The more serious aspect of settlement occurs when the bricks begin to part and cracks appear in the mortar. Again, this need not be disastrous. It may never move again. If you see that the bricks themselves have cracked, then the matter is more serious and, if the house is visibly leaning over, it is very serious indeed.

You may see that someone has already filled the cracks with more mortar and yet the crack has obviously continued to move. In such a case, there is really very little that can be done to save the property.

Another problem which has become more frequent, in recent years, due to the more general use of solid floors, is the tendency for them to settle on the supporting fill, beneath. You will see that this has happened when the floor has dropped an inch, or so, below the bottom of the skirting board.

All these points are serious, to a degree, but can usually be cured, providing the settlement has stopped. You will only see that if repairs have been made and the crack not opened up afterwards. If in any doubt, leave the house alone.

It is always sensible to ask the owner what work he has done to the house, recently. Much of it will be obvious; new decorations, for example, can never be hidden and should always be treated with suspicion. Just what are they covering up?

One particular point to cover is the electrical system. If the house was built before the last war, look out for plug points. If they are all of the square pin design, then the system has probably been renewed and rewired. If they are still the old round type then the system is the original one. It is probably highly dangerous and the chances are that you will be faced with a complete rewiring, in the not too distant future.

When you visit the roof space, look out for any wires that pass across the joists. Do the same in the cellar, or when you lift a floor board. There was a bad tendency, a few years ago, to use a cheap, two-element wire, for domestic electrical systems. You should never find it in more modern houses; the rules of safety are much too tight. You can find it in older houses. If you discover that use has been made of such materials – usually two wires, twisted together, like a rope, and covered in a blue or a brown, cloth-like covering – you can be sure that some rewiring is essential.

Finally, look at the plumbing. Modern systems use copper pipe and its presence indicates that the pipe work is fairly new. If there are old lead pipes, then be prepared for some repairs. They may be in excellent condition. They may very well not be.

Particularly look out for any signs that lead pipes have been connected to copper, or plastic. This is a good indication that the work was done by a bodger, not by a tradesman.

And do not forget to look at the outside plumbing. It is remarkable how few people bother to look at the gutters and down pipes, on the outside walls. In fact, the expense of having them repaired can be surprisingly high. Bear it in mind. Remember, also that leaking gutters can cascade water into the fabric of the house and store up all the dampness problems which we have already considered.

When you have completed your examination, decide whether you will want to do the repair for yourself, or call in a builder. If the latter, ask the owner's permission for the builder to call and give an estimate. If the owner refuses to allow this, forget about his house.

Armed with the builder's price, or your own list of work to be done, you are nearly in a position to bargain over the price of the house, itself. Before you begin, however, there are one or two more points which you may well be advised to check and think about.

7

Other Hazards

You read earlier that the house owner is no longer immune to attempts to take his house away from him. A whole assortment of bodies have the legal authority to acquire all, or part of his property, whether he likes it, or not.

However, we live in a democracy and there are safeguards. The bodies who enjoy such powers are all firmly under the control of Parliament, who require a very good reason for giving such authority to anyone.

The only reason for Compulsory Powers – as they are called – being used against any house owner, is the general good of the whole community. The rules are quite clear, that he should be properly compensated and, on the basis explained in Chapter Two, that property is only one of the ways in which you can 'store' your capital; if you are paid for it, even compulsorily, your capital has simply been changed from one form to another, as explained. The only difference is that, this time, you were forced to do so, whether you liked it, or not. If only it were quite so simple.

Although complicated arrangements exist simply to make sure that justice is done, not everyone feels satisfied with the final result. Added to this, a point must arise where the inconvenience caused to you is beyond compensation.

We all of us have to accept a degree of risk that our property may be affected by some future planning scheme. For the house buyer, however, the position is much clearer. There is no reason at all why you should get into such a position, with your eyes open. With a few, simple questions, you can avoid a lot of problems.

Any proposal which the Council has already decided to implement, will be known to the Planning Officer, at the local Council Office. Visit the office and ask for the Planning

Department. Explain to the officer who interviews you that you are considering buying a house – give him the address – and you would like to know if there is any likelihood of a re-development scheme affecting the property.

His answer will take one of several forms.

He may confirm that there is a scheme and explain just how far the house will be affected. He will also give you some idea when it is likely to happen. If the proposals entail the eventual acquisition of all of the property, then you are best advised not to buy it. On the other hand, if they mean that you will only have to give up part of your garden – often the case where road improvement is planned – then you must judge for yourself, whether this is acceptable to you. A couple of feet of ground cut off the end of a front garden which is a hundred feet deep, anyway, is hardly a disaster. The Road Authority will put back a proper wall, in any case. Remember, however, that, once a scheme has become a firm one, requirements tend to increase.

If the Officer says that there are no schemes, ask him if the house is in an area where there might be, at some future time. He will generally give you a shrewd indication of the possibilities, and, once again, you must be the judge.

He may tell you that the property has been, or may be 'represented as unfit' by the Medical Officer Of Health, and, in this case, you must be very careful. A 'represented house' is technically a 'slum' house, and, in the old and popular expression, is 'Condemned'.

Should this be the case, you should leave it alone, at all costs. When the time comes for action to be taken, you may find yourself required to pay for the demolition of the house and left with a useless piece of ground. Or, if the Council decide to buy it off you, the house itself will be judged to be worthless and only the land will be bought from you, at land value. As most older houses stand on plots which are far too small to take a modern house, that value will be almost nothing. Worse, if you have a mortgage, you may find yourself without a house, receiving only site value and left to repay the original mortgage, in any case.

Of course, the officer may say that there are no schemes and, so far as he is aware, no likelihood of any. This puts you back to making your own assessment.

Look at the house again, in general terms. Is it old or new? A new house is much less likely to be represented as unfit, but could be included in a road improvement scheme. Is it built on a busy road?

It is a good idea to stand outside the house, between five o'clock and six, in the evening. You will see, then, how the traffic builds up and whether there are delays and hold-ups. If there are, the time may come when the Council must widen the road. How near will that bring the road to the house? Remember that this will not simply be a matter of loss of land. The road itself, with its traffic fumes and pedestrians on the pavement, will be brought closer to your front door. Perhaps even more annoying, they will also be brought closer to your front windows.

And now, look at the area in which the house stands. Quite apart from anything else, a new, modern house, built in an area of older, less desirable houses, is always a problem to sell. People who can afford that sort of house usually seek it in a better area. You should only pay a price which allows you to re-sell later, without loss.

You read earlier that a new house is unlikely to be represented as unfit. This is true, but, where a council has a great many unfit houses and they decided to acquire the area for redevelopment, they have the power to acquire fit property which is so placed as to make the area difficult to re-build.

Taken a step further, the Council also has the right to acquire whole areas of fit houses, where the overall good of the community would be better served by re-development. This is particularly the case in areas which are sometimes described as the 'rotten ring'.

People with money tend to build themselves larger houses, on the edge of the towns in which they work. In London, this has reached the point where they are living in areas thirty to fifty miles from the centre. A hundred years ago, they were content to move to the rural delights of Battersea and Hackney.

As communications developed and people moved further out, these areas became less fashionable and the large houses, in their big gardens, became worth less and less. Many were converted into flats – of varying standards.

Clearly, the ground on which they stand is being seriously under-used and the Local Authorities have the power to acquire such properties and re-develop more efficiently.

The re-development itself might be new housing, a new school, a hospital or similar. No one could deny the need for these things but people do lose their homes as a result. You are advised to avoid getting into such a situation, in the first place.

If the Development Plan, in the local Council Office, shows the area as being zoned for a new school, or a similar public building, even if no firm scheme has been announced; or if the house is in an area of large, older houses which are generally run down; then beware of possible clearance.

If the house, in which you are interested, is itself an older property, you must consider whether it may be represented, in due course.

The popular idea of what constitutes a 'slum' property is a semi-derelict, occupied by dirty, illiterate tenants. In fact, to the Medical Officer of Health, whose job it is to represent the property, the word slum means something much more specific.

In law, a slum property is one which lacks certain basic amenities, where those amenities cannot be easily installed. This means that a house which has been well looked after and is, to all appearances, in good condition, may still be represented as a slum. It might have no Damp Proof Course; it may have no proper ventilated storage for food; it may have no water supply or modern sanitary arrangements.

There is no reason to bore you with lists of reasons why a house may be represented as unfit. It is enough to say that any older property, short on the amenities which are now regarded as normal, in a modern house, could, possibly, be represented.

In fairness, if you do find yourself owner of a represented house, you may be entitled to what are called Owner Occupier's Payments, or to 'Well Maintained Payments'. However, in practice, all the extra payments put together are most unlikely to add up to the price which you paid for the house in the first place.

Not all the problems of position arise from local planning

policies. Some are the result of human activity, in the area.

For example, unless you really have no alternative, there is little to be said in favour of living in an old, traditional mining area. Years ago, mining was carried out very much closer to the surface than is now the case. At the same time, all too often, they were not so careful as they should have been, when it came to keeping maps of what they had been doing.

The result is that you can seldom find out if there is any danger of your house being damaged by subsidence. Subsidence is very much more serious than the settlement described earlier and, if you have reason to suspect it, you are strongly advised to go elsewhere.

When you visit some houses, you may notice that the road in front of the house, is not surfaced – at least to the standard we expect from a 'public' road. This is particularly common where the house is still being built. If this is the case, you should make a few inquiries.

First of all, was there a gate at the end of the road, to control traffic; or a notice saying 'Private Road', or similar? Or, when asked, does the Vendor confirm that the road is not maintained by the Council? If this is the case, be careful.

Years ago, people liked private roads on the estates where they lived. It allowed them to control who might enter their demesne and gave them greater privacy. They had to accept the cost of maintenance, of course, and the cost of a man to open the gate or bar unwelcome visitors. In practice, the people who chose this way of life were generally wealthy and putting their hands in their wallets for such a modest cost presented no problems.

Nowadays, the position has changed considerably. Costs of maintenance and staff are very high and few people can be so open handed. People purchasing houses on such roads should realize that they face one of two possibilities. Either they will continually be paying higher and higher maintenance charges, or they will find that no one will want to chase the others for their share of costs and the road will deteriorate for want of attention.

They face another danger, too; but this is more common

with the other type of unmade road. The ordinary un-surfaced, 'unadopted' road. These are those rough roads which the Council have not yet taken under their wing.

Apart from the problems of broken car springs, and the more modern phenomenon of people who think that an unmade road is provided for them to use as a rubbish tip; the big danger is that the Council may decide to adopt it. If they do, they have the right to require all frontagers to make it up and surface it to their standard. In practice, most people, faced with such a situation, let the Council do the work and charge the costs of them. The point is that these costs may run to several thousand pounds.

As if that was not bad enough, there is another problem. Building Societies are terrified of road charges and, where there is any risk that such charges may become due, they will generally retain a sum out of the Mortgage advance to cover the cost. This reduces your mortgage advance and com-plicates your finances generally.

Of course, all these problems will be discovered by your Solicitor, later, but as the facts will have a considerable bear-ing on your decision about buying, or not, there is a lot to be said for knowing sooner.

Ask the Vendor, and ask at the Council Surveyor's Office, if the road is adopted, and be warned if it is not.

There is one type of house which is almost certain to front on to an unmade road. That is the one being built on an estate. Normally the Developer agrees to make up the estate roads, as part of the sale contract. As the building process involves the use of heavy equipment, it makes sense to leave the road making until the house building is completed, rather than be continually damaging the surface.

This is fine, providing the Builder does not go bankrupt and fail to keep his agreement. If he did, you would find yourself paying the Council to make the road up, even though you may already have paid the Builder.

If there is any risk of this happening, the Building Society will, again, retain a sum to cover the cost, but, in most cases, there is a better answer.

Most Councils will only give planning permission if the Builder will agree to deposit the cost of a road making, with them, or to take out an insurance bond, either of which will indemnify the Council if they have to step in and make the road up.

If this has been done, the cost is covered and you have nothing to fear. You can check the point by asking the Council Surveyor if the Builder has a 'Section 38 Agreement' with the Council. If he has, all is well. If he has not, then bear in mind the risks which you are taking.

Say in note what this is.

Very few people can resist the thought of living by a river. The idyllic prospect of looking out of your bedroom windows, at the gentle waters and the green willows; of fishing from your own lawn; of mooring your own boat at the garden end; what could be nicer?

Very little, and it would be wrong to over estimate the disadvantages, However, disadvantages do exist.

Low lying areas, adjoining rivers, are all too often damp. The atmosphere can be unhealthy, even if it never actually becomes foetid. Anyone who suffers from rheumatic or bronchial troubles, should think very hard before going to live there.

Even more dramatic, is the possibility of flooding. Most major rivers flood; some annually, some even more frequently. When they do so, they can flood many square miles to a depth of several feet. People living in the area either move out or move upstairs. Soon, the floods recede and life goes back to normal.

All a jolly adventure, you say? Not as a regular occurrance. Those of you whose experience of flooding is limited to the odd burst pipe, with its nice, clean water which dries out quickly, can have no idea of the filthy mess, left behind by a flooding river. This is not the pure content of the crystal stream. At least half of it consists of the industrial waste, spilled oil and untreated sewage of most of the towns further up river. If you want that in your house, each year, good luck to you. If not you are strongly advised to check any possibility of flooding with the locals. You can then make your own assessment.

Living by the sea does not seem to have the health hazards of living by a river. On the contrary, it can be very helpful to those who, in the old phrase, 'enjoy bad health'.

You will be told that breathing the ozone is responsible

but, what people really breathe is the far less polluted air of our coasts, constantly refreshed by sharp sea breezes.

Flooding is seldom a problem, in coastal areas. Where it is – generally on the East Coast – it is in areas which have been reclaimed from the sea. Local inhabitants will be quick to tell you their flood stories and, again, you must decide for yourself.

If there are disadvantages in living on the coast, they arise from its popularity. In any coastal resort, the shop prices tend to rise in the Summer, and you can be very much inconvenienced by visitors who insist on parking their cars outside your gate. Having a sea view, and living on the sea front, is not so pleasant if you cannot get your car out of the garage for half the Summer.

For this reason, there is something to be said for living half a mile or so from the sea front. Of course, even this will not discourage the many people who suddenly remember what good friends they were to you, in your old home town, just at the same time that they decide that they would like a free holiday.

The aim of this chapter has been to show you that many things, outside the house, outside the site even, can affect your enjoyment of it. What has been pointed out is all fair comment and you are advised to consider the points raised. On the other hand, you cannot hope to allow for every possible contingency. A factory, which you cannot even see, can pump out smells which you only notice in certain weather conditions. You will only know if the neighbours tell you, and they may well be exaggerating.

Listen to them; make inquiries; but, in the end, make up your own mind.

8

The Decision, and After

So you have decided.

You have considered all the pros and cons. You have talked it over with your partner and you are happy about the condition of the property.

Or is there still some small difference of view between you. It is by no means unusual and is solved surprisingly easily.

The best solution for couples who are not entirely in agreement about the purchase of a particular property, is to let the person who will spend most time there make the final decision.

If one of you will be working from home or spending a great deal of time there looking after young children, then let that person have the ultimate say in the matter. It will affect both of you if one partner is not happy with the surroundings.

So now you really have decided. What is the next step?

First of all, have you decided to pay the asking price or to make an offer? This is really judged on two points. Firstly, can you afford to pay the price being asked and, secondly, is there any risk that someone may come along with a higher offer? For reasons which we will explain, there is likely to be a period during which neither you nor the vendor are finally committed to the sale. In practice, far more purchasers pull out than vendors, but you are always at risk, to a degree. If you think that there is a risk of someone offering a higher figure before contracts are settled, you may find it easier to agree to pay the asking price.

Which ever you decide, telephone, or call on the Estate Agent and formally make your offer. If it is the asking price, he will almost certainly be able to accept, there and then. Otherwise, he must take instructions.

On this last point, if he is to do his job properly, he must put any offer which he receives, to his client. It is always tempting for an Agent to push the interests of a purchaser who has another house to sell, and is prepared to instruct that particular Agent to sell it for him. Two fees are always better than one.

Again, this is not to suggest unspeakable villainy on the part of every Agent. Only a few fall for such temptation, but you may find one of them.

The answer is to hand the Agent a letter which confirms your offer, and to send a copy of the letter to the Vendor of the house. If the Agent does what he is supposed to do, no harm will be done. If he does not, the Vendor will be aware of the situation. Always describe the offer, in the letter, as being made 'Subject to Contract'.

One point of misunderstanding may arise from the Agent's duty to tell his Client of all offers he receives. It sometimes happens that, after one offer has been accepted, another, higher one is received. If the owner decides to cancel his acceptance of the first and go on with the second, it is quite unfair to blame the Agent and claim that he should not have submitted the second offer. He has no alternative. In any case, he does not accept offers. Only the Vendor can do that, and the Agent simply does as he is told.

You will now enter a period of bargaining; long or short, according to your anxiety about losing the house. The offer you will make reflects the costs of repairs which you know are required and, at this point, you must not lose sight of the total expense which you face. You may need furniture, new curtains and the rest. Husband your resources and do not over-reach yourself.

The Agent may want to check that you really can raise the mortgage that you claim you can, before putting the offer to his client. This is quite reasonable. His duty to his client is to advise him of your ability to go through with the purchase. If you refuse to be frank with him, he is right to assume that something is phoney.

If and when your offer is accepted, you will call at the Agent's office and give him the details which he requires in order to instruct Solicitors to prepare a contract.

He will ask you for your full name and address, and that

of your Solicitor, and this is a useful point at which to explain just what a Solicitor is, and does.

A Solicitor is the Lawyer who, under English law, acts in the preparation of contracts and conveyances of property. The law regarding property ownership is complicated and generally beyond the comprehension of anyone not trained to understand it.

This is not a Lawyer's plot. A moment's thought will show that, by its very nature, land ownership is unlike the ownership of anything else. If someone offers to sell you a hat, it is not unreasonable to assume that he owns it and is empowered to sell it. The fact that a person is occupying a house is not proof that he owns it, at all. He may be a tenant, or a leaseholder, pretending to be a freeholder. For that matter, he might be a squatter.

In addition, so many things can affect land which are not obvious, immediately, that, in order to avoid misunderstandings, ownership is usually evidenced in written documents called deeds. These prove that all the persons who have ever sold the land, had a legal right to do so, and that the land passed to each person fully and legally. The deeds should also give an indication of any rights over the land which are enjoyed by other people. These could include rights of way, rights to lay drains in the land, and a whole range of others.

It is probably true to say that our English system of passing round great bundles of ancient documents is rather outdated. There is a case for the continental system of registration of interests and transfer of ownership at the Town Hall.

In fact, the Land Registry is an attempt to introduce such an arrangement but it does not yet cover the whole country, and has never reached the point where the transfer of land has been simplified.

For all practical purposes, we are stuck with our bundles of deeds.

You may ask, could you check the deeds for yourself? There is no legal reason at all why you should not, but have you ever read a legal document? Would you understand it, if you did?

No, if there is any case for a person, involved in land

conveyance, not instructing a qualified professional, it can only be when the person concerned is selling. He only has to answer questions. If you are buying, face the facts. Instruct a professional.

Few Solicitors will decline to act for you. You will be paying them a fee and that is what they are in practice for. However, common courtesy suggests that you should check before you give any Solicitor's name to the Agent. It entails no more than telephoning his office and asking if he will act for you in the purchase of a property.

Since Solicitors are now prevented from using fixed scales of charges, there is no reason at all why you should not telephone several and ask for an indication of his fee for conveyancing a house of such-and-such a value, and comparing one with another.

Until recently, only Solicitors were allowed to charge for conveyancing. But, now you can employ a Licensed Conveyancer instead. These are people who are either former Solicitors, qualified Solicitors' Clerks or others who have a minimum of ten years' conveyancing experience and have passed the conveyancing and accounting examinations. New entrants must complete at least two years' practical training and pass the appropriate examinations. Then they are allowed to establish their own firms after three further years.

All Solicitors and Conveyancers must be insured against dishonesty and negligence. Solicitors also have their own complaints procedure; if you believe you have been over-charged, you can ask the Law Society to check your bill. All Conveyancers who belong to the National Association of Conveyancers have to comply with strict rules of conduct and could be disciplined by the Association if these rules are broken.

After asking for the name of your Solicitor/Conveyancer, the Agent may ask for a deposit. This is a sum of money, part of the purchase price, which is paid to him as an act of good faith on your part. In the past years, this was usually ten per cent of the agreed price, but, as the average mortgage became a larger proportion of the cost, nominal deposits of fifty and a hundred pounds became usual. Nowadays most Agents do not bother with deposits as the administration of them is too time-consuming and costly. But if your Agent does, when he gives you a receipt, be sure that it contains the magic words 'subject to contract'. If it does not, ask the Agent why.

This phrase enables either you or the Vendor to withdraw from the deal, at any time, up to the signing of the contract and – most important – reclaim your deposit. A great deal can emerge, in the period before the final signing. Your Solicitor will use the time to check out all the facts and important considerations and will only allow you to sign a contract, and finally commit yourself to the purchase, when he is entirely happy with the purchase.

He may well find a defect in the title which will allow you to withdraw, even after signing, but the majority of these problems are small and would be matters for damages rather than your pulling out altogether. By using the phrase 'subject to contract', you are able to withdraw without giving a reason, if it seems best that you should.

Some sales are agreed which are not subject to contract. Occasionally, you will be asked to sign a contract immediately, in the Agent's office. If you do so, and it is up to you, you may only withdraw at the risk of being sued for any loss which the vendor makes as a result of your withdrawing. You will also lose your deposit.

There is another situation in which you sign a contract immediately. That is, at Auction. The whole question of buying at auction is dealt with, in the next chapter.

Once the Agent has all the information he requires, things begin to move quickly. He will write to the Solicitors and, generally, provide yours with a copy of the deposit receipt. It does no harm, however, for you to call on your solicitor and confirm that you have gone ahead with the purchase.

You should now make your formal application for a mortgage.

Go to see the Building Society Manager. He will ask you to complete a form, with his help, if you wish. He will also ask you for the Society's Surveyor's fee. Now is the best time for us to look at the different types of mortgage which you can consider.

There are now many alternatives to the straightforward repayment mortgage on offer: endowment mortgages; low initial repayment mortgages; escalator mortgages; fixed interest mortgages. If you are confused by the choice, ask your Building Society Manager or financial adviser to explain the differences between these mortgages and help you choose the type most suited to your situation.

The ordinary repayment mortgage is one of the most popular types of mortgage. Put simply, the loan will be repayable, over an agreed term, at so much each month. The interest will be variable by the Society, during the term, but you can rely on the Management to restrict increases as far as possible.

Endowment mortgages have become very popular over recent years. They require you take out an endowment assurance which will provide, either on a fixed date or at your death, if this happens first, a sum of money which will pay off the mortgage loan. You then pay interest only to the Building Society.

Until the 1984 Budget, income tax allowances were received on both interest payments and insurance premiums, but not capital repayments. So, for the higher tax payer at least, a mortgage which combined insurance premiums with interest payments gave him a bigger tax allowance.

Unfortunately, the tax allowance on premiums was removed in respect of policies agreed after the Budget date and the endowment mortgage is now less attractive than it was. It may still be cheaper for the younger purchaser but you must ask the advice of your Building Society Manager or other financial adviser.

Insurance brokers may well be keen to persuade you to take out endowments but be on your guard. They earn commission on sales and their judgment may be a little influenced as a result. Always compare the TOTAL cost of the endowment mortgage with the alternative repayment mortgage.

But there are still a few shots left in the Insurance Agent's locker. He will suggest that, by paying a 'little' extra, you can change your Endowment into a 'with profits' policy and, at the end of the period, pick up a sum which will not only clear the loan, but will, in effect, repay all the interest which it has cost you, over the years.

As already explained, that interest is simply the owner occupier's version of the 'payment' which we all make for living in the house. All that the Insurance Agent is doing is

selling you a Life Assurance policy. Pay him so much a
week and he will pay you so much, in so many years' time.

Now, nobody is suggesting that life assurance is not a
sensible thing to have. On the contrary, only foolish people
would ignore the need. But, tying it to house purchase may
not always be the best course. If you want to have a sum
equivalent to the total interest which you have paid, then,
you can always take out an endowment assurance policy,
and keep it separate from your mortgage. Shop around, and
look for the cheapest policy you can find.

Finally, the Insurance Agent will point out that, should
you die before the end of the term, the endowment will pay
off the loan in any case, and remove the burden from your
surviving partner.

True, but a repayment mortgage can be covered, quite
cheaply, by what is called a Mortgage Protection Policy.
This will do exactly the same.

There is one final word of warning. In times of mortgage
shortage, the only possible way in which you can get a
mortgage may be through the good offices of an insurance
broker. If you are in a hurry, the extra cost may be worthwhile.

Mention of the tax allowance on interest paid to a
Building Society raises another point. It used to be up to
the borrower to claim this allowance on his annual tax
return. Nowadays, however, the basic rate allowance is
made by the Society asking you to pay a little less than the
full interest due, and by their then claiming the balance
direct from the Inland Revenue. This system is called
MIRAS, standing for Mortgage Interest Relief At Source.

For most people this is a simple arrangement and calls
for no action on their part. Complications arise, however,
where the borrower has a mortgage of more than £30,000.
Interest on borrowed money higher than that figure does
not have a tax allowance. If you are borrowing that sort of
money, seek the advice of the Society Manager or of an
accountant.

Once you have applied for your mortgage and paid your
surveyor's fee, you simply wait for the result. It will take a
week or two to arrive. You must be patient. On the other
hand, if you find yourself still waiting after three weeks,

telephone the Building Society Manager, and ask what is happening.

During this time, you should understand that you have no more than a gentleman's agreement to buy the house. Either you or the vendor can withdraw if you or he wishes, and he can sell the house to someone else for a different price. The process is sometimes known as 'gazumping' and causes great annoyance to its victims.

In fact, few people seem to understand the problem. A purchaser who has agreed to buy 'subject to contract' has reserved the right to withdraw from the contract. He can hardly complain if the vendor has and exercises the same rights.

People who call for the outlawing of 'gazumping' are really saying that one party to a contract should be bound by his word but the other party not. That simply is not fair.

The best way to avoid being 'gazumped' is to sign a contract immediately and few purchasers wish to do that.

In the meantime, your Solicitor has already started work. We will take a look over his shoulder and see just what he is doing.

9

Legalities

While you have been looking after your mortgage application, your Solicitor should have been hard at work. A few words to explain just what he does, will help you to understand his part in the procedure.

The Estate Agent will have sent him a letter explaining that you have agreed to buy the house and giving him the Vendor's name and that of his Solicitor. It would be wrong of your Solicitor to accept this, without checking the facts with you and, if you have not confirmed your wishes to him, he will write to you and ask you to do so. This is why it is always a good idea for you to call on him and warn him to expect the Estate Agent's letter. It saves time.

Once he knows that he may proceed, the Solicitor contacts his opposite number who is acting for the Vendor. He, in turn, sends to your Solicitor a document known as the Abstract of Title. This is a boiled down version of the Deeds and gives all the details which he will require, in order to satisfy himself that the Vendor does have the right to sell the property and that there are no problems. There may well be difficulties which you could not know about but which would have given you second thoughts about buying the house, had you known. If there are any points which disturb him, he will raise them with the Vendor's Solicitor and advise you just what is your best course.

In his own words, he is checking to see that the Vendor has a good 'title' to the property. He wants to be sure that the title goes back to a good 'root'. This is some piece of evidence which is old enough and clear enough to be beyond any dispute and which shows all the subsequent documents to be reliable.

He will also make 'searches'. These entail writing to the various authorities who might have plans or knowledge which would affect the house. These include Local Councils, Land Registries and a number of others. Sometimes these are slow to reply.

When he is happy that all is as it should be, he prepares a contract and, in due course, invites you to sign it. The Vendor signs a duplicate copy and an 'Exchange of Contracts' is arranged. This simply means that each Solicitor hands over the copy he holds to the other Solicitor and, from that point both you and the Vendor are committed to go through with the transaction, or be sued for failing to do so.

This is important. Obviously you will not wish to sign the contract until your mortgage application is settled and, in practice, this means delaying until a written letter of mortgage is received from the Building Society.

If in doubt, rely on your Solicitor's advice.

On exchange of contracts you will have to make a deposit of ten or five per cent of the purchase price (or increase the deposit paid to the Agent accordingly). If you are putting in more than ten per cent from your own money then there is no problem. If not, then you should ask your Solicitor what you should do. Some Solicitors will lend you the money until the mortgage is paid over to him but others may suggest that you approach your Bank Manager.

If you do, and show him the letter of offer from the Building Society, he will usually be able to help you.

Once there is a contract in existence, the transaction is no longer subject to contract. If you withdraw, after exchange, you will certainly lose your deposit and, possibly, risk being sued, at the same time, for any loss which the Vendor incurs, when he resells. Be under no illusions. The time to change your mind has gone.

Of, course, you now have the advantage that the Vendor is also committed and that the price of the house is, in most cases, fixed. There is, as always seems to be the case, one exception.

In the case of a contract with a Builder, you will be very lucky if you can get him to tie himself to a price, on a house which is not yet completed. This is not entirely unreasonable. Materials do go up in price and some room for manoeuvre is only to be expected. All that you can do is make a mental note that the price may increase, before completion. Where the contract states that any increase will be to cover increases in labour and material costs, make sure that your Solicitor has a full statement of just how these are calculated before actually paying them. If they seem rather high, you can take the advice of an independent Building Surveyor.

Builder's contracts often call for another item which may frighten you. Stage Payments. These are payments made to the Builder, as the work proceeds, and cover the cost of what he has done, up to that point. There is no need to worry about these. When the builder asks for a stage payment, simply pass the request to the Building Society. Their Surveyor will make another inspection and, if he is happy, authorize the Society to pay the sum out of the mortgage already agreed. You will have to pay a small fee for each extra inspection and will also be expected to pay the interest on the money which is advanced to you. All this is perfectly normal.

In theory, once contracts are exchanged, your Solicitor will be handed the deeds of the house, on loan. He can now check that the abstract was accurate. Solicitors belong to a very tightly controlled profession and fiddling with abstracts, in order to mislead a purchaser, is so clumsy that it is most unlikely that a Solicitor would be stupid enough to try it. It would be very surprising if the deeds told a different story from the abstract.

At this point, you should make certain your new property is insured against fire. This is because the contract will still exist, even if the house burns down, before completion. You could still be required to buy it, even though it is gone. The small cost of the insurance is well worth the protection it gives. At least you will not lose your money.

The contract will normally contain a date for the 'completion' of the purchase. This is the great day when the money is paid, the deeds handed over and the house becomes yours.

A few days before completion, your Solicitor will ask you for a cheque to cover any money still due from you. He will obtain a cheque from the Building Society for the amount of the Mortgage.

On the day itself the money is paid over to the Vendor's Solicitor; the authority to retain the deeds is handed over to yours, together with a new deed. This is signed by the vendor and acknowledges that he has passed ownership of the property to you.

If you are borrowing any of the money, the deeds are then passed over to the Building Society as their security.

Although this sounds terribly complicated, it is really not so. In practice, the vast majority of house sales go through without any problems at all. Of course, there are always exceptions which do not follow the rules, and we will try to explain these and what you should do, if you find yourself in such a situation.

The first variation which may arise is the refusal of the Vendor, or his Agent, to deal on a 'subject to contract' basis. He may ask you to sign a contract in his office, immediately and pay a deposit.

If he does, you should refuse. Never sign anything without your Solicitor's advice. If you do, you will find yourself losing your deposit if you withdraw for any reason other than a serious defect in the title deeds. The fact that, subsequently, you cannot raise the mortgage is not good enough reason to avoid loss of deposit and, possibly, legal action for additional loss.

There are so many houses for sale, on a subject to contract basis, and the alternative is so unusual nowadays, that there is often a sinister reason for anyone wanting to tie you down so quickly. There is an exception to this. In Scotland, subject to contract procedures are rare. You buy your house direct from the Lawyer and sign in his office. If you are buying in Scotland and see a house which you like, you may find it wiser to see another lawyer before committing yourself. He will protect your interests – for a fee, of course.

In England or Wales, the original advice holds good. If they want you to sign a contract on the spot, bid them good day and leave.

You may occasionally come across a half-way house system. This is particularly popular amongst Builders, who will require a purchaser to sign a sort of pre-contract and pay them a 'holding' deposit. This is forfeitable if you withdraw before the full contract is signed. The Builder will normally undertake not to sue you in addition. Very kind of him. It is up to you if you are prepared to do business on this basis. At least you know what your loss will be.

Builders justify this system on the grounds that it discourages time wasters. Perhaps it does. I doubt it.

The last example of a 'not subject to contract' sale is perhaps the most interesting. <u>Sale by Auction</u>.

The popular fear of bidding at auction is completely un-justified. The Auctioneer will not try to force you to bid a figure which you cannot afford; nor will he claim that you blew your nose and must buy the house. The whole business is too important and serious for such silliness. You can bid up to your top price, without nervousness. On the other hand, if you prefer, <u>you can get another Estate Agent to bid for you.</u>

Auction is chosen for the sale of a house, for one of three reasons. Either the property is too unusual for anyone to be very sure just what it is worth; there has been so much competition for the house that an auction, with its atmosphere of rivalry, is obviously going to persuade people to pay the most that they can afford; or the sale is such that the Vendor must be able to show that he made every effort to get the best price possible for the property. This arises where the Vendor is acting for someone else. For instance, as Executor under a will.

Vendors do not choose to auction properties lightly. For reasons which you need not bother about, auctioning a property is much more expensive, for the Vendor, than selling by private treaty.

The point to remember is that, if your bid in the saleroom is the successful one, <u>you will be asked to sign a contract and pay a ten per cent deposit, there and then. This means that you have to make all your arrangements for mortgage</u> before the auction.

In practice, the three or four week period of advertising prior to the sale, allows you to do just that. Go to the Building Society Manager and explain that you propose to bid for a house, at auction. He will allow you to apply for a mortgage and will do his best to ensure that you get your offer letter before the auction date.

<u>The Auctioneer will be able to show you a document, known as the Conditions of Sale, and the abstract which we have already</u> discussed. This may tell you all you wish to know about the property but it is not a bad idea to ask your Solicitor to look at it for you. He will advise you whether to **bid, or not.**

At the auction you should try to keep your head. The highest bid which you can afford to make will be the mortgage which you have been offered plus the money which you can find for yourself. Never be tempted to bid higher. The time available for you to find the extra is just not long enough. If the bidding goes beyond you, accept the fact with a good grace.

At the auction, stand at the back of the room. This enables you to see who else is bidding and to gauge the amount of interest. If it is clearly flagging, you can always offer the Auctioneer a bid lower than the one which he is asking for. He may not accept it, but there is always a chance that he may. Why pay more than is necessary?

If you have never attended an auction of property before try to go to one or two, before the sale of the house which you wish to buy. This will give you an opportunity to learn how the Auctioneer works; how his patter runs. By doing this, you will see how to avoid embarrassing mistakes, such as bidding against yourself.

In this respect, do not confuse a property auction with any other sort. Cattle Sales, Furniture Sales, vegetable Marts, and certainly Cheapjacks at the seaside, are as unlike a property auction as chalk is from cheese. You will learn nothing to assist you at any of them.

Delays before Contract

People buying their first house can be excused for not knowing how long it should all take. Obviously it is dangerous to generalize, but, roughly five weeks up to exchange of contracts, followed by another four for completion, would be normal. This could be longer, of course, if you or the Vendor have another house to buy, or sell, and want to settle both deals at once.

It would be longer, also, when the house has yet to be built.

If you hear nothing from your Solicitor for three weeks, it is quite reasonable for you to telephone him and ask for a report on progress.

When you are selling one house, in order to buy another, you can help to shorten the process by putting your own house on the market quickly and making sure that your Agent, if you have one, maintains the pressure.

As the great day draws nearer, you may wish to re-decorate the house, or do one or two repairs. You must ask the Vendor's permission, of course, and if he gives it, he may require you to sign a receipt for the key which states that it is lent 'for the purposes of viewing only'.

This is quite reasonable. Once people have possession of a house, even illegally, they are difficult to get rid of. Even though they pay no rent and refuse to complete the purchase, the procedure for removing them can be an annoyingly long one. Of course, if you do any work in the house, before completion, and then withdraw, for any reason, there will be no compensation for you. On the contrary, you may be required to pay the cost of putting the house back to what it was, before you started.

And then, suddenly, it's here. The day when you become a householder, with all the problems which that entails. If you have followed my earlier advice, you should already have insured your new property. If not, you must do so now. Remember the house is yours and if anything happens to damage it, you will be the loser. You will still have to pay the Building Society its money back. You may find that the Society will insist on insurance, in any case, but, if not, it is up to you.

Moving your furniture in is best left to the experts. If you try to do too much, you give them the excuse that any breakages which occurred were the result of your interference. Confine yourself to telling the removers just where you want things to go. They will do the rest.

If you are having carpets fitted, arrange for the fitters to come a day or two later, or earlier. Carpet fitters require a lot of space and there just is not room for them and the furniture removers to work at the same time. The same goes for builders and decorators.

When they have all gone and life seems to be getting back to normal, you will be able to sit back and look over the events, trials and troubles of your move with a sense of achievement.

And now your future in your new home lies before you. Good luck.

10

Selling — Estate Agents or Do-it-yourself

It does not require a genius to work out the reason why anyone should wish to sell his house without the help of an Estate Agent. He hopes to avoid paying a fee.

Many people feel that the usual fee, paid in such circumstances, is too large for the work that the Agent actually does.

Having been involved with property for more than twenty years, I know something of the costs that an Agent has to meet, if he is to run his business properly. Believe me, they are far higher than you would think and the position is made worse by what the Agent will call 'abortive work'. That is, the work that he has to do for nothing.

If a house does not sell, its owners do not expect to pay a fee; notwithstanding the fact that the Agent will have incurred expenses by offering the house for sale. The result is that the Agent must recoup the costs from the Vendor whose house did sell.

I am the first to agree that this simply is not fair. But, it is the system that has grown up. No one can blame you for trying to avoid that sort of fee.

In case you feel that it is strangely altruistic for a property man to be advocating 'do-it-yourself' house selling; that I am effectively taking the bread out of my own mouth; let me say this. My motives are not strictly altruistic at all.

Most Estate Agents will agree that unsold property, cluttering the market for weeks and weeks, simply depresses sales for everyone. There will always be those who prefer to do things for themselves and it is far better that they do them properly and avoid causing problems for other people.

Out of those who offer their houses for sale, privately,

there will be those who are successful and those who are not. Of those who are not, many will be forced to call in an Estate Agent. All too often, he will find himself having to pick up the ruins of good but misinformed intentions. All too often any chances of a sale will have been wrecked before he arrived on the scene.

By following the advice which I have set out, you will stand an improved chance of sale but, if you are unlucky, you will at least be able to go to an Estate Agent without having already made mistakes which will make his job impossible.

Before starting on any enterprise, it always pays to learn something of the background to the problems you are likely to face. The background to house ownership is very much like the majority of other things. It has changed considerably, in recent years.

Fifty years ago, the few house owners probably knew the local Estate Agent socially. There would only be one, or, at the most, two Agents in the average town.

Prospective vendors went to him as a professional man, for his advice. They would rely on him. He would advise them on price and handle all the difficulties with total self-assurance.

Nowadays the Vendor usually has a wide choice of Agents in his area. He is unlikely to be on more than nodding terms with any of them and he goes to them, not for professional advice, but because he wants a sale.

Far from wanting advice on price, Vendors will often tell the Agent what they expect him to ask. Far from relying on his professional ability, many Vendors put their house on the books of every Agent in town. The fact is that they are not seeking a professional service. They want brokerage. The simple introduction of possible Purchasers to possible Vendors.

Estate Agents have accepted this trend and many have adjusted their approach to business in order to provide what people seem to prefer. Every town, nowadays, seems to have its modern, expensively furnished establishment, where smart suited salesmen try to persuade purchasers that 'this is the one for you'.

This is inevitable and has not yet reached the end of its

course. People, nowadays, have a pretty fair picture of what they mean by the word – salesman – and they do not see why Estate Agents, selling houses, should be very different to motor dealers, selling cars.

In fact, as most house owners today are people in modest circumstances, they generally prefer to discuss their business affairs with a sympathetic salesman, rather than a highly qualified, socially elevated professional.

All this complicates the decision which a Vendor must make. No longer is it simply a choice between 'do-it-yourself' and appointing an Agent. You must now decide between the professional Agent and the brokerage Agent, as well.

Let us try to weigh up the arguments on each side.

The vast majority of Agents are honest men, trying to earn a living by providing a service. The few cases of serious malpractice, which do reach the newspapers, are indicative of just how infrequent such occurrences really are. Newspapers never report regular happenings. They gave up reporting every little road accident years ago.

The chances of you being swindled by an Estate Agent are very remote and, if that is your only reason for not instructing one, it is not a very good one.

The choice which you face is firstly, between instructing an Agent, or not and, secondly, between a professional Agent and a Broker/Agent.

If you are in any doubt about your ability to do the job for yourself; if you are leaving the district quickly and will not be available to do the detailed work, then appoint an Agent. Far better to do so before any damage is done.

Agent or Broker? Again, it varies with the circumstances. Generally a professional Agent is likely to be more thorough and a Chartered Surveyor is, by his qualifications, a man whose knowledge of property has been tested and who has passed some stringent examinations. The unqualified Agent is likely to find himself in difficulty if the sale turns out to be a legally complex one, while the Chartered man should be able to sort out the problems with ease.

On the other hand, the vast majority of house sales go through without any problems at all.

In the end, the decision can only be based on the local standing of the Agent concerned. Your friends will soon tell you all the lurid tales about each Agent in town and this provides some indication.

Getting an Agent to act for you is remarkably simple – on the face of it. You select the Agent you prefer, telephone him and ask him to sell your house for you. He will call round, measure it up, agree terms with you and set about the job of selling. If indeed it was as simple as that, there would be few problems. However, there are a number of pitfalls for the inexperienced.

When the Agent calls, he will note down the information he wishes to pass to possible buyers and then advise you on the price. If he is clearly trying to fish for the figure which you are prepared to accept, be on your guard. He is there to advise you – not simply agree with your idea of price. You are more likely to be wrong than right. Stick at him until you get *his* figure.

If you do not agree, there is no reason why you should not say so, providing you can say why. Perhaps an identical house, nearby, sold for a higher figure. Tell him so.

He may well be able to explain just why that was the case. Always feel free to discuss the price, logically and in the light of facts which you understand to be true.

There is no point in simply disagreeing with him, without evidence to back you up. If there are no clues to the value, the question becomes one for expert opinion. That means his, not yours.

And now the complications begin.

Agents do not work for nothing. Neither do you. There will be a fee to be paid, in due course. It is as well to know what it is, before you instruct the Agent so that there are no misunderstandings, later.

Now, ask him whether he will be charging for advertisements, in addition to his fee. Again, this varies from one part of the country to another. If he does charge separately, arrange that he spend up to, say, £200 and then speak to you before incurring more expense.

In the end, you will probably have to allow him to spend more, but it does mean that you retain some control of the situation.

The vast majority of Estate Agents rely on word of mouth agreements but some may produce a 'form of instruction' and ask you to sign it. Be careful. Check what you are signing.

The form may give the Agent 'Sole Agency' for so many weeks. This will mean that, should you appoint another Agent, within that time, who sells the property, you will have to pay a fee to the first Agent, for doing nothing, as well as a fee to the second.

'Sole selling rights' are even worse. You will be paying a fee, even if you sell the house, yourself.

Some Agents will ask for a fee in advance. Others will ask you to agree a fee, whether they sell or not. A minute's thought will show you the unreasonable nature of such an arrangement. If the Agent can collect such a fee from ten or a dozen house owners, each week, he need never actually sell the houses, at all.

Britain is full of straight-forward Estate Agents, prepared to deal for you, without complicated selling contracts and to wait for their fee until the sale is completed. There is no need to work on any other basis.

If the Agent asks for an advance fee or produces a 'sole selling rights' contract, show him the door. If he sends you a bill 'for advice' send it back and suggest that he sues you.

If he wants you to sign a 'sole agency' contract, restrict the contract period to one month. This, at least, will prevent too long a delay.

The whole question of 'sole agency' is complicated. In some areas, no one appoints more than one Agent. In others, chiefly the larger towns, everyone goes to every Agent in town.

The argument in favour of multiple agency is that you get a full coverage. In fact, house seekers invariably visit every Agent in the area, in any case. The chances of your house not being seen by a purchaser, because you instructed one Agent only, are very remote.

If you instruct ten Agents, each one knows that he stands no more than a one in ten chance of earning the fee. Is he really going to try very hard or will he prefer to push the house for which he has a sole agency?

Perhaps more seriously, multiple agency destroys the

chance of a proper Agent/Principal relationship and makes
the Agent even more of a Broker.

It sometimes happens that a Sole Agent fails to sell a
house and the owner feels bound to bring in other Agents.
The first Agent will probably offer to instruct the others, 'to
save you the bother'. If he does, politely decline. He will
offer them a shared commission basis, which means that
they have a ten to one chance of getting HALF commission.
This is even less attractive than the earlier suggestion.

Always arrange that, should there be any question
of additional Agents, you will instruct them direct. Not
through him.

Once the property is advertised, whether through an
Agent or privately, you may be approached by other
Agents, touting for instructions. Ignore them.

Some people think that touting shows enthusiasm. It does,
but not where it should be shown – in looking after the
interests of existing clients. It shows enormous enthusiasm
for turning a quick fee. Agents who have good selling
records are usually too busy to chase business in this way.

It is significant that the Agents who go in for touting are
usually those who want to tie you up, hand and foot, with
sole selling contracts and fees, whether they sell or not.

People will come to inspect your house surprisingly
quickly, once the Agent leaves. This is because he will
usually telephone those possible purchasers who he thinks
will most like your house.

They will almost certainly be polite and complimentary
but do not read too much into their reactions. Nothing is
going to be gained by your telephoning the Agent, after each
visit, bubbling over with enthusiasm. If they want the house,
they will say so.

After three weeks, if no sale has been made, have a con-
ference with the Agent. Remember that, in the end, the only
course open to you is to reduce the price of the house, until
someone thinks that it is worth it.

When you do at last sell, there are still a few points to
watch.

The Purchaser may have a house already, and need to sell
it before he can buy yours. Your Agent may be instructed to
sell that house, as well. In one sense this is a good idea. He

retains full control of the situation. He will know if there are problems and can advise you accordingly.

On the other hand, it is awfully tempting for an Agent to take on a second house sale, in this way, knowing that it is overpriced and simply hope for a miracle. You are the one who will be inconvenienced in these circumstances.

If the buyer of your house is obviously having problems in selling his, take the opportunity of driving past it, one evening. If you think that it is over-priced, ask the Agent to explain. You may be wrong and he may have a reasonable explanation. If so, no harm is done. He will realize that you are not going to be trifled with and that is a good thing.

After a month, when it is clear that your purchaser is having trouble, tell your Agent to re-offer and inform the purchaser of your decision. There is no reason why he should not still buy the house, if he can do so in time.

Time is the one thing which you cannot waste. Never let other people waste it for you.

If the last few paragraphs have given the impression that relationships with Estate Agents are fraught with peril, I am sorry. The bulk of all property sales are trouble free. Few people have any reason to regret appointing an Estate Agent, apart from the fee.

But we will assume that you have decided to go ahead and do-it-yourself and, as an initial guide to the best system to adopt, the next chapter tells you just what an Estate Agent does when he takes on the job of, offering a house for sale.

The system is well tried and provides a sound base from which you can work. There is little to be gained by ignoring it completely or trying revolutionary ideas of your own. Time is short. Leave experiment to those who are sufficiently experienced to know when the experiment is not working.

11

The Process of Selling

When an Estate Agent takes on the sale of a house, he does several things, almost at the same time. Broken down, they are as follows.

He advises on the price.

He prepares written details, photographs and advertisements.

He sends details to all those people on his list who have asked to be informed of the sale of houses, more or less similar to yours.

He submits advertisements to all those papers and magazines which he considers are best suited to your type of house.

He will accompany people who show interest, to your house and show them all over it. This gives them a chance to see what is on offer, but allows you to know that your property is protected while they do so.

He gives details of the house to anybody who inquires at his office.

He will put a card, advertising the house, in his window and possibly a photograph as well.

When an applicant decides to buy, the Agent will know what questions to ask, so as to be sure that the purchaser will be able to raise a mortgage, assuming that he needs one – most people do. This will avoid any delay while the property is 'off the market'.

Finally, the Agent will instruct the Solicitor you have appointed, providing him with any other information which he needs to know.

And, now you are saying, 'My Agent never did all that for me, when I sold my last house'. If that is the case, all that can be said is that he jolly well should have done. In this increasingly competitive age, more and more Agents are learning that only those who give a proper service have any chance of survival.

The list which you have just read, provides a guide to all the things that you must do for yourself, and later chapters will deal with them in detail. Before we move on to consider them, there are one or two things which allow you to prepare the ground.

First of all, however, just a few words about the decision which you had probably made before you bought this book. The actual decision that you propose to sell.

You may feel that this is an unimportant detail. Either you are going to sell, or you are not. What more is there to be said?

Rather more than you may think, in fact.

Experience shows that there are a remarkable number of our fellow citizens who take some strange pleasure in offering their houses for sale. Note the word – offering. Seldom do they reach the point where they actually sell.

One dear old lady once asked me to put her house on my books because it would bring visitors for her to talk to. It was all rather sad but, even though she was an extreme case, there are people who are not much less so.

Either they like the opportunity to show off their homes to others or they want a conversation point. They will often justify their efforts by saying that, if they get what they think is a fair price, then they will go and look for a new house. They never do. The truth is that they do not really want to sell at all.

Any Estate Agent, worth his salt, soon gets to know the regulars and how to recognize the latest entrants to the hobby. He can take evasive action but the general public is rather more at their mercy.

Oh yes, you may say, but it is your money. If you want to waste it on pointless advertisements, then it is up to you. This may be partly true but there is another side to the matter.

The people who come to view your house will be seeking a new home. Some of them will be rapidly reaching the end of their tether with the frustrations of the business. It simply is not fair to encourage their hopes that their search is over, when, in reality, you are not really serious about going through with it. There is always a very real danger that, while you are misleading them, they could miss the opportunity of buying another house which would have suited them and where the Vendors were not indulging a very selfish whim.

If your house is too big, or too small; if you are moving to a job in another district, then these are fair reasons to be selling. Trying out the market for fun is not.

It boils down to this. Be sure of your motives. It is only fair to other people. In any case, remember the fable of the boy who called wolf.

One further piece of advice. Many people like to instruct an Agent on the basis that they will pay commission if he can find a buyer, but not if they find one for themselves.

Be advised. It simply is not worth it.

It always finishes in arguments over who actually found the purchaser.

Most people seeking a house will contact all the local Estate Agents and your Agent will always be able to make a case that he gave the purchaser details of your house, even if you feel that you did all the work. In any case, no Agent likes to be in competition with his own client.

Either give the job to an Agent, on a proper basis, or do it yourself. There is no satisfactory half-way arrangement.

Are you still sure in your own mind that you want to go ahead? If so we will move on to the next stage. That is preparing the ground in order to make the final job much easier.

The first thing which you must do is to let your Solicitor know of your intentions and to tell him that you will be writing to let him know the name of your purchaser, as soon as you know who he is. This will give him an opportunity to clear his decks. He will obtain your Title Deeds from where ever they may be, and then prepare his draft contract and other papers.

Next, notify the Manager of the Building Society with whom you have your mortgage. Better still, go and see him. Tell him your plans and make a point of asking him if the eventual puchaser will be able to get a mortgage from him.

He can only answer in general terms. So much will depend on the purchaser, himself. He will be able to warn you if funds are so short that no mortgage is likely. Even if this is the case, it is not the end of the World. Your purchaser may have a source of his own.

Before leaving the office, obtain a pamphlet, giving the repayments necessary for a range of various mortgage advances. Put it in the file which you should have already opened, marked 'house sale'. Almost every Society publishes such a pamphlet and it will be invaluable, in due course.

Also ask the Manager if the Society takes into account, any, or all of a partner's salary in their calculations. The rules vary from Society to Society.

If the Society rules ignore the second income, the Manager will usually tell you the names of Societies who do not. There is no reason why you should not obtain pamphlets from them too.

The information will help you to advise prospective purchasers and ease the way to a sale.

Gather all the information you can, particularly information on repayments.

On the way home, buy a copy of each of the more popular local newspapers. Inside you will find the address of the Advertising Manager. This too, you should add to your file.

You are now ready to start the real work of selling. The next chapter tells you how to go about the first problem.

Deciding just what is a fair price, for your house.

12

What Price?

Without any doubt, the most difficult question which you will have to answer, during the whole exercise of selling your house, is – what should I ask in the way of price?

This is not because it involves some complicated formula, but because we are all too much involved with our own property to make a completely unbiased assessment.

Even after many years in the property business, most Estate Agents jib at the thought of valuing their own houses. They usually arrange for a friend to do it for them.

And yet, even that has its dangers. A real friend will not wish to offend you and may tend to be kinder, in his figure, than he should be. A complete stranger is often far more likely to give you the proper advice which you are seeking.

You could avoid the problem of valuation, if you wished, by paying a Valuer to do it for you. But his fee is likely to be high and, in any case, most 'do-it-yourself' purists would feel that paying for advice, in this way, smacks of cheating.

Only you can decide but let us assume that you wish to do your own valuation and explain the best way in which to go about it.

But first, before we can even begin to think about actual figures, there are a number of pitfalls which you must understand, otherwise your calculations will be entirely pointless.

The first problem is the biggest. It amounts almost to a mental blockage.

Get it firmly into your thinking that your house is not made worth a penny more, simply because YOU happen to live in it.

In case you think that that remark is rather obvious, be warned. We all fall into the same trap, at least to some extent. We all rationalize it, of course. We tell ourselves that we paid £2,000 to have the garden laid out, mentally adding £3,000 to the price. We remember the Vinyl wallpaper in the bathroom and add £250 for that, and so on.

Put yourself in the other man's position. The garden may not even be planned in the way which would suit him. An enthusiastic gardener will want to lay it out in accordance with his own ideas. The man who hates gardening will shudder at all the weeding; that is, if he even looked at the garden at all.

How much Vinyl wallpaper did you use? Ten rolls, eleven, perhaps? And how much did it cost? Ten pounds a roll? You would have spent about £4 a roll, in any case, on paper. This means that the extra cost was really no more than £50, or £60 at the most. Does that really warrant an increase in the price of the house? Particularly when you have had a year or two's use of the paper, anyway; and the purchaser will almost certainly tear it all down and replace it with paper of his choice.

The brutal truth is, and you may just as well accept it, that, if the house next door sold for £60,000 last week, it is pretty certain that yours will sell for very nearly the same price, this week.

It makes no difference at all that the other house was dirty and that the owners had dubious visitors. A good clean-up will deal with the dirt and the former owners' morals are the last thing that any purchaser is going to be concerned with.

There are a number of other mental blockages to be overcome and these are best illustrated by a short story.

Bob and Mary are very friendly with Tom and Joy. Bob and Mary lived in a semi-detached bungalow, while Tom and Joy lived in a four bedroomed house, set in two acres of ground and paddock. They are, nevertheless, all good friends.

Tom and Joy decided to sell up and move to another house which had caught their imagination. They sold their house for £150,000. Bob and Mary, influenced by their friends and their example, also decided to sell. Unfortunately, their pride would not allow them to ask a price which would amount to admitting that they could only afford a smaller property than their friends.

They asked a silly, unrealistic figure. They did realize this but, somehow, they just could not face the truth.

And the result? Months later, they had still not found a buyer. In an effort to avoid losing face before their friends, they had created a situation where they had made themselves into laughing stocks. They had forgotten completely that real friends are not interested in the value of the house in which you live. They are interested in you.

Once again, the moral is – BE REALISTIC. There is no shame in being poor, unless it is brought about by your own improvidence, or is just in your own mind.

A particular difficulty which you will have to face is that you are not just calculating one figure. You have to decide on two. They are, the price which you will ask and the price which you will accept.

It has long been the custom that the purchaser of a house will try to 'get a bit off the price'. It is equally the custom that vendors react by 'putting a bit on, first'. Of course, this makes nonsense of the whole procedure, but it is the system that has grown up, almost as a ritual. Like so many other rituals, that achieve nothing, many people would be happy to see it finished with. It makes no difference. There is nothing to be gained by rocking the boat. You may only sell two or three houses in a lifetime. It is better that you accept things as they are.

But, having said that, just how far apart should the two figures be? Experience teaches us two things, in this respect.

It is true – as you are sure to be told – that you 'can always come down, but you cannot go up'. If you carry that principle to the ultimate extreme, you finish up asking a million pounds for something which you are really prepared to sell for fifty pence.

This may seem a silly example but it makes the point. If you increase your asking price to a much higher level than the house will justify, those people who can afford it will not buy because they will know that they are not getting value for money. On the other hand, those who could afford to pay a fair price, and no more, will not bother to inspect a house, so obviously out of their price range.

The other important point to remember is the 'thousand

pound barrier'. These are the enormous mental hurdles which face people who are asked to pay a price above the limit which they are working to. The average home seeker will set himself a limit of so many thousand pounds. Ask him to go above it and you will find that he becomes most unhappy at the idea. Many Estate Agents will tell of the man who refused to inspect a house, which was priced at £50,050 because it was over his 'limit'.

All too often, he goes on to buy a house for something like £49,995. Fifty-five pounds less. What makes such a situation worse is that, in many cases, the owner of the first house would not have refused an offer of £49,950, and that the house would probably have suited the buyer's needs, at least as much as the one which he bought.

By far your best course of action, in such circumstances, is to put a little on the price, to allow room for a reduction, but to limit it to a hundred pounds, or so. If that hundred pounds raises the price beyond one of the 'thousand pound barriers', set the price just below, even if it is only five pounds below. There really are people who pay prices like £44,995.

Another warning. Far too many people base their acceptance price on a calculation involving the price which they are being asked to pay for their next house. It is quite pointless, as a moment's thought will show. The two things are entirely separate, and yet, every Estate Agent has heard, time and time again, those same, tearful words, 'But we've GOT to get £50,000'

If your house is not worth it, you will not get it.

Finally, ignore those friends who assure you that you ought to get 'at least another thousand, My Dear'. They mean well. They are trying to be complimentary, but they are seldom valuers. Ignore them, as well as the other friends who will assure you that they got so much more for their almost identical house. They are boasting.

And now, armed with a whole array of 'don'ts', you are ready to go.

First of all, have a drive around the area and note all the houses, similar to yours, and which have Agent's boards outside. Then go round the Agents, gathering up the particulars of these, and any others which they may be offering and which sound as though they might also be similar to yours.

Do be realistic. Stick to those houses which are quite honestly, like your own. Self deception, at this, or any other stage, is completely pointless and only serves to make the job harder.

When you sort them out, some will obviously not be good comparisons after all. Throw them out.

Of the remainder, an examination will show that there is a definite level of values, with the majority of the properties being priced somewhere near to it. There will be a few which are priced much higher, but if there are no obvious reasons – luxury kitchen, double garage, etc. – ignore them. The owners are falling into one or other of the traps against which you have been warned.

Now you will be left with your reasonable and acceptable comparables, and the general level of asking price will be clear. Note – asking price, not selling price. The latter ought to be somewhere between 2% and 3% less.

If you are disappointed, then forget the whole thing. Do not be led into an expensive and time wasting experiment which is never going to achieve anything, anyway.

13

Telling Them That It Is for Sale

Unless you let people know that it is for sale, no one will buy your house.

You have a choice of several means of making the fact known and we will deal with them all, in turn. You may not wish to use them all but that will not matter. Not all of them will necessarily suit every house.

First of all – Sale Boards

This is by far the simplest method for drawing attention to your house and is always to be recommended. You would be surprised how many people do really ride around, on a Sunday afternoon, looking for houses with sale boards. Only when they have found the one which they really like the look of, will they contact the owner.

The board can say, quite simply, 'For Sale', but your little boy has only to leave his bicycle, on the ground, within fifteen yards of the notice, for it to cause all sorts of complications!

To avoid this, 'This House For Sale', is much better. It is personal, obvious and virtually idiot proof, in what it has to say.

Some Vendors like to put something extra, such as 'Full Central Heating', or 'Four Bedrooms'. It is entirely up to you, but there is a strong case for keeping the message as simple as possible. People are seldom completely stupid. They can usually gauge whether a house has four bedrooms or two. If you have a real selling point which is not obvious, then do put it on your board, if you must, but do be sparing in your praise, if you do not want to appear silly.

Other people prefer to ask viewers to make an

appointment. Again, this is a matter of choice, but generally, it is probably safer nowadays if you include on your For Sale sign, 'Viewing by appointment only', and give your telephone number. This makes sure that you get any applicant's name, address and telephone number before sending him any details about your property. To ensure he has a genuine interest in it, ask him to ring for an appointment after having seen the details.

There are few things more off-putting than a roughly made, old notice, written on a shoe box lid and looking as though a dozen rain storms have soaked it. How can people seriously imagine that purchasers are going to be attracted by such an object. To most it has the opposite effect.

It is such a pity, especially when there is no need for it. A reasonable board is not a difficult thing to produce. If you have any talent for painting, you are home and dry, but, even if you have not, there is a simple answer which will produce notice boards, capable of passing the sternest critic.

Buy a piece of Hard-board from your Do-it-Yourself Shop. It should measure approximately 18″ × 30″. At the same time, get two pieces of self adhesive plastic sheet. The shop assistant will be able to advise you. Buy two colours – white and blue, or white and red – it does not matter as long as they are in strong contrast to each other. A yard of each will be sufficient.

Stick one piece to the smooth side of the hardboard, following the maker's instructions on the backing sheet. Never rush it. It will only spoil the final job. Wrap the surplus round the edges of the board, to make a neat finish. It also helps to keep the rain from getting between the board and the plastic and spoiling the board. You now have a board with an all over coloured base.

Now, decide on the size of the letters which you propose to use. Aim to make them big enough to be readable but not so big as to confuse the eye. Having decided the size, and using guide lines on the backing paper, cut the other piece of plastic into strips of the same width as the height you want for your letters. This helps you to keep your letters all at one height.

And now, cut the letters from the strips, again using the guide lines on the backing paper.

Draw light pencil lines on your base board, using a ruler, of course. These will be the guides for your letters. Remember to draw them as guides for the top of the letters, not the bottom. Arrange the letters on the board, so as to balance the design reasonably, and then start to stick them down.

This is best done by turning the top corner of the backing paper on the rear of each letter. Just a tiny bit pulled away so as to expose the adhesive.

Place the letter on the guide line, holding it down to the board by finger pressure on that part of the letter which still has its backing paper in place. When you are satisfied with the lie of the letter, push the exposed adhesive, in the corner, down on to the board, fixing it permanently at that point. Slowly peel the backing paper away from the fixed corner, easing the letter down as the adhesive is exposed. With care, you will produce a board which will compare with anything that you could buy.

And now, particulars.

You are strongly advised not to try to produce 'Agent' style particulars. You will obviously wish to give applicants some information, but these should be straightforward details and no more.

There are two reasons for this.

Firstly, Agents are experts. They know just how far they can go in the way of purple prose. This is doubly important, since the passing of the Trade Descriptions Act. You will not know where to stop and you will risk getting yourself into very hot water, as a result.

Secondly, people will accept an Agent's fulsome description, but they will only laugh, if you try writing it yourself. Remember that you will be describing your own house. If modesty fails to prevent you overdoing it, think of those roars of mirth among your friends. That will be much more salutory.

You can do no better than to prepare something like this:

For Sale – Freehold (or leasehold, you will know which)

23, Ensor Drive,
Wattlingstone,
Barsetshire.

Situated one mile from the town centre and within ten minutes walk of the local shop and 'bus services, the house was built of brick with a tiled roof, some ten years ago. Accommodation comprises:

On the Ground floor.

ENTRANCE HALL with power point, LOUNGE (10′ × 23′) with power point and fireplace. DINING ROOM (10′ × 11′) with power point and TV aerial point, KITCHEN (12′ × 11′) with stainless steel sink unit, range of fitted cupboards and stores, power point, cooker point, gas point etc. etc.

Deal with the first floor in a similar manner. Try to avoid adjectives like magnificent, spacious, unique and all the rest. The garden can be 'laid out with lawns, flower beds, paths, etc.,' but only if it really is. It is always best to avoid descriptions like 'tastefully laid out with formal lawns, known throughout the country for its spacious, flowered arbours, sylvan walks—' and so on.

Be careful to avoid obvious nonsenses, such as indicating that the garage is in the kitchen. It has been done before. Beware of the term 'double garage'. A real double garage will take two cars, but some people are inclined to get a little upset if you use the phrase to describe what ought to be called a 'tandem garage'. That is, one in which one car is parked in front of the other and then requires the movement of one in order to get at the other. Better say 'garaging for two cars'.

Complete your statement, so:

Electricity, gas, mains water connected.
Price required £— Freehold (or leasehold)
Viewing by arrangement with Mr. —— at Wattlingstone (0660) 654321.

If you have a telephone line it may be referred to. However, the line is not yours to sell. The instrument(s) also belong to British Telecom unless you have had the line adapted with the special sockets. Say 'Telephone connected, subject to B.T. regulations'.

And there it is. Simple, accurate and adequate.

The Press is by far the best media for the publicity which your house will require. Not just the Press, generally, of course, but that section of it that is properly chosen to suit the type of house which yours is.

But, before we consider the choice of newspapers, just a word about the type of advertisement which you should choose.

There are two types of press advert, as far as we are concerned. They are the Display and the Classified. Agents make use of a half-way house system, in which their general advert is a large Display, with the individual houses included within it, as what are, in effect, classified adverts, but under the Agent's display heading.

This means that, for practical purposes, most houses are put in as classified advertisements, but some warrant something a little better and may even be good enough for display with a photograph.

Once again, be warned about lack of realism. If your house is quite unique, and particularly attractive, or if it has some point so worth showing that only a photograph will do it justice, then go ahead, but again, a warning.

Photography, and in particular, architectural photography, is an art and it is far easier to make a bad picture than a good one. Added to that, nothing holds back a sale like a poor photograph, so do be selective.

You can pay a photographer, if you wish, but even he cannot do the impossible.

The situation is made worse by the fact that some delightful houses simply refuse to show up well in a photograph, while others, often appalling old ruins, photograph very well indeed. You will see immediately that you are on a loser, either way. A good photograph of a bad house will annoy all those who rush to see it and are disappointed by it. A bad photograph will discourage them from coming to see it, in the first place.

The display advertisement, without a photograph, is really an expensive waste of effort. Proportionately, it costs far more than the classified. You might think that a classified advert risks being lost amongst the hundreds of others, while a display will stand out. In fact, the display is just as lost and people seeking houses usually read every advertisement, anyway. *Set local papers in area chose to live in*

On balance, the classified is to be preferred every time. That is unless a photograph really is worth inclusion. The classified, without a photograph, is simpler to lay out, cheaper and gets the same results, in ninety-nine cases out of a hundred. You will gain little by doing anything else.

Wording the advertisement is not so difficult as it may at first appear. Simply include the important details, but without any silly adjectives. For example:

'For Sale. Freehold. Detached bungalow, elevated position. Five minutes walk from shops and 'buses. Lounge, Dining room, Kitchen, two bedrooms, Bathroom/W.C. Full oil-fired central heating. Garage and shed. Front and rear gardens. Price required ——.
Details phone——'

Something on those lines will do the trick. If you say too much, then people will jib at what seems to be gilding the lily; say much less and they will not be able to see just what it is that you are selling.

Some Vendors use a box number, when advertising. It is up to you but, generally speaking, it is questionable what benefit there is in this. The applicant has got to know your address, sooner or later. Why make it harder for him. You will never keep the mere sightseer away, if that is what you hope to do. That type will not be put off by so small a difficulty while the real buyer may well be. In any case, have you ever tried to sort the genuine from the false from a few words, spoken over the telephone?

Your choice of newspaper depends almost entirely on the house itself. In country districts, most houses respond to advertising in the local weekly. In the larger towns, there is usually a local daily and you should make use of it.

You will recall that you already have the name and

address of the Advertising Manager of your local paper, on your file.

If you are selling a larger, country style house, you may decide to advertise in the local County Magazine. Most counties have one and, by purchasing a copy at your local newsagent, you will find the address to which you should send advertisements. Do check the price of the advert, before sending it. You may be somewhat shocked by the cost.

There is no need to repeat the warning about realism. Just try to remember it, when you decide to advertise in any of the 'glossies'.

Some magazines are specialist in certain fields and there may be a case for the odd advert, where your house is likely to interest the readers. A house over-looking a harbour, for instance, or owning a boat mooring, can be advertised in the Yachting press quite successfully.

If you live in an area which is dominated by a large, national firm, with a good turn over of employees, all moving in and out of the area; it may help to advertise in the company's staff magazine. Probably, one advertisement, as a tester, would be enough to make the point. The same can be said about an area which has a large public body based within it. Civil Servants need houses, too. You can advertise in the Staff Association Journal, generally on quite reasonable terms.

For the address of the magazine, write to the Secretary of the company, or the Establishment Officer of the public office, concerned, explaining your request. They are most unlikely to refuse to help.

When submitting your advert to any paper or magazine, you may find that there is a reduced rate if you book two or three insertions at once. By all means take advantage of this. You will be very lucky indeed if you sell after only one insertion. Even if you do, you should be grateful enough not to grudge the extra cost. Book at least three insertions,

You may have noticed that some shops, particularly newsagents, have a card box, on a wall, outside. In this box people can insert cards, for a modest fee. You can put your house advert in as well, although the value is questionable. The range of items and services advertised in these boxes is often more a cause of hilarity than sales.

In practice, no one seriously seeking property, goes fumbling through the '1962 Marmite Prams' and the 'attractive young lady – French lessons given at reasonable prices' when they are looking for information.

However, the card box does have the advantage of being a cheap form of publicity so you may be tempted to use it. You can use the same word layout as in your newspaper advertisement.

After three weeks of newspaper advertising, you should review the situation. Bashing on regardless, with no sign of a sale, is just silly. Think the matter through, particularly in the light of comments made by those people who have been to see it. Have you failed to stress a good point? Or over-stressed a bad one? Examine the newspaper again. Is it the right one, after all? Do those people who are most likely to buy your house, actually read that paper?

Finally, think about the price. When all else has failed, the price is the only thing that you can change. You can never put the house into a better locality, or add bedrooms. You can only offer it a little cheaper.

- ET
- citizen
- Herald & Post

14

Showing It to Best Advantage

People will only buy a dirty house at a dirty price. No doubt you can work out for yourself just what a dirty price is.

What, on the other hand, is a dirty house? The expression covers a great many things; bad repair, lack of paint, uncultivated beds in the flower garden, old, rotting wallpaper and – rather obviously – dirt.

Sometimes it is no more than a veneer of dust, doing nothing worse than taking the shine off things. At other times, it is a revolting heap of filth, rotting on the floor. It can also be that even worse, grimy, greasy look that so many of us find the most off-putting of all.

It is remarkable the number of people who cannot be bothered to clean up their house before putting it on the market. Of course, if the property looks dirty and gives the impression that it has obviously not been well cared-for, prospective purchasers will not feel inclined to make an offer. It is only common sense and in your own interests to make every effort to clean your property if you want to be successful in selling it!

So the moral is – give the house a good clean.

Untidiness is not dirt, and many, respectable and otherwise clean people can be very untidy, leaving all manner of things, simply lying about. Children are always obvious, not so much by their presence as their chaos. Do try to have the place in some semblance of order, if people are going to visit you.

Of course, some evidence that the house is lived in, is inevitable, but there are limits. Heaps of ironing in the chairs; breakfast things, unwashed in the sink at tea time; books, strewn around the floor: all these things go beyond them.

People are genuinely put off by chaos, unreasonable though it may seem.

The inevitable question is, whether one should redecorate the house, prior to sale, or not. Estate Agents are used to being told that the Vendor proposes to 'do' this room and that room. In practice, it is usually a total waste of time. Almost everyone, on moving into a new house, will redecorate, as soon as their finances will allow. Your choice will seldom be the same as theirs and they will certainly tear down all that you have put up.

The only circumstances where redecorating is advisable are where the decorations are really grubby, as opposed to faded. Anything else simply costs money and has little bearing on a purchaser's final decision.

So much for the house. What about you?

Again, people are not entirely unreasonable. They know that you have to go on working, and even living, while your house is on sale. They will not mind you having your tie off, or your carpet slippers on, but they will look a little old fashioned if you are still in your dressing gown, after lunch.

Not only your personal appearance but your whole attitude can make or mar a sale. People can call at the most inconvenient times and you will lose a chance of doing business, if you are in any way off-hand with them. If it is genuinely inconvenient to allow them to inspect; if you have guests or are just on the point of going out, smile sweetly, tell them the truth and try to arrange an alternative time.

On the other hand, do be sure that your reasons for doing so are genuine. If in doubt, give your visitor the benefit and let him in.

Always remember that they are doing you a favour in coming to see the house that YOU wish to sell. You are not obliging them in any way. With this firmly in mind, you should find that a co-operative attitude comes to you, naturally.

No one expects to be allowed to wander, at will, through your house but try to avoid dogging their heels, as though you suspected their intentions for the family silver. Try to retain the initiative. Escort them, guide them. Do not simply follow them.

They will rush through some rooms and tend to linger longer in others. Let them.

Let them see what they want to see in their own time.
Most of them will be complimentary about various things
they see. Never be misled into the trap of believing that this
means anything at all. In fact, the more complimentary they
become, the less likely is it that they will buy the house. No
one is going to make rude remarks about your property,
even if they think that it is terrible.

If you are drinking a cup of tea when they arrive, offer
them a cup, but do not feel under any obligation to make tea
for them deliberately. You are trying to sell your house and
attempting a little modest bribery, for that is what you will be
doing, will not help. Only a friendly, honest attitude, a tidy
house, combined with a sensible price will ever do that.

Never enter a room and promptly reel off a long list of the
advantages that it offers. Let them react first, and then add a
very few, quiet comments, giving the impression that you
are agreeing with them and not pressurizing them.

If their eyes wander towards an obviously bad point, get
in quickly with some comment, such as. 'There was wood
worm in the window frame, but we had it treated and we
have not been troubled since'.

Be prepared with your list of items which you propose to
include in the sale price or which you are willing to sell, in
addition. The Purchaser may well prefer to delay his decision on these points, until he has decided whether he wants
the house, or not. When he does decide you will have to
make your mind up just how rigid you wish to be on the price
of items, in the light of how desperate you are to sell the
house itself.

Last of all, if it is a couple who are viewing, leave them
tactfully alone, when they have seen the house. They will
want a few words together, before making a decision.

15

' Well, We Like It '

These are, without doubt, the most wonderful words that anyone selling a house will ever hear. They are the one bit of encouragement which you are likely to receive. Of course, it can be completely changed by the next sentence, but it does mean that you have created some interest.

The applicant may well follow it with one of several phrases. We will try to cover each one and tell you how best to counter it.

'—but we can't afford it.' '—but it is too far from the school/shops/'buses.' or some such comment, are all quite obvious. Whether they are being honest or just trying to let you down lightly, it does not make any difference. They are not going to buy.

You can always make some comment about being prepared to consider a lower offer, but, usually the decision is already quite firm in his mind and has not been based on price, in any case. Let him go.

'—but I could only offer £xxxxx.' This is an easy one to deal with. If it is above the price which you have already set as your acceptance, you know what to do.

Either suggest an intermediate price that you will accept, or accept his offer. You will decide which, in the light of how long the house has been on the market, or how desperate you have become. People expect to haggle and you must haggle back, or you risk them beginning to wonder if the house is such a bargain, after all.

If you are not happy at the thought of haggling, then you should have gone to an Estate Agent in the first place.

'—What do we do next?' This means, almost certainly that they will buy at your price. Sit down and set about the formalities. Now is the time to put the kettle on.

But now, a sad story.

An Estate Agent once sold a house to an applicant who

told him that he would be selling his own house, privately. It was his decision. There was no alternative but to let him get on with it.

After a month, the owner of the house which he had agreed to buy, began to get a little restless.

'Had the purchaser sold his own house?'

'No.'

'Why not?'

The Agent did not know and agreed to find out. He was rather conscious that he had not exactly done his job properly and went, rapidly to see the purchaser. A forlorn sale board stood in the garden and it was a very forlorn purchaser who met him at the front door.

It appeared that he had sold his house, the day after he had first advertised it. He had not re-advertised, but had learnt, a fortnight later, that his purchaser could not get the mortgage that he required, on his salary. He could not, therefore, proceed with the purchase.

Sadly, the owner put his advert back in the paper, and, lucky man, he sold again, within a few days. Having had his fingers burnt once, he waited a fortnight, and that very night, had been to see his second buyer. He had learnt that this man too, could not get a mortgage. He had known this for ten days, but had 'thought that the Vendor would have guessed, as he had heard nothing'.

The moral of this sad story is simple. Both the Vendor and the Purchasers honestly thought that the job of finding a mortgage was the least of their worries. In fact, it was their greatest. The point is that any Estate Agent who knew his business, would have known that both possible purchasers would turn out to be non starters, within two minutes of meeting them.

How? Quite simply.

The maximum mortgage that someone can raise is always governed by his income. The Building Societies are always anxious to avoid the embarrassment of taking foreclosure action where borrowers have failed to keep their payments up to date. It injures the nice image that they have of the house purchaser's friend. As a result, all Societies adopt rules which decide the maximum sum which they will advance. In most cases, this is as follows.

They will lend you approximately two-and-a-half to three times your main gross annual income, plus once any second income.

These amounts will always depend on your personal circumstances and, of course, although these figures were correct at the time of writing this book, the Building Societies may change them whenever they like in the future. Check with your own Building Society to find out the maximum they will lend you.

Let us take an example. Joe and Mary hope to get married soon and want to buy a house together. Joe earns £10,000 a year and his fiancée also earns £10,000. They have a sum of £10,000 saved up in the Building Society. Their Society lends three times the main income, plus the second income, which means that Joe and Mary will be able to borrow £40,000.

The couple are advised to put £800 of their savings on one side to cover legal costs and so by adding their possible loan to the cash they have available, we can tell that the maximum which they can afford to spend on a house is £49,200. They are strongly advised to restrict their search to houses within a short range of this figure.

Remember that the Building Society will work on Joe and Mary's gross salary, not their salary after tax and other deductions. They will have to find out from their Building Society what their monthly repayments are likely to be; they must make sure they can afford to pay these amounts, bearing in mind any other expenses they have.

There is another complication. If the Equity, that is the amount which Joe and Mary are putting in from their own money, had been less than ten per cent of the cost of the house, they could have difficulties. In times of mortgage shortage, the Societies tend to limit their advances to ninety per cent or even less of the valuation of the house. Joe and Mary, therefore, need a ten per cent stake, at least; possibly a little more, because the Society's Valuer may well value the house at less than the asking price. In such a case, they will be required to make up the difference themselves.

This last point is important. Building Societies are not run by fools and they will always send a qualified Valuer to report on any house put up for mortgage. This means that there is no hope whatsoever of your getting more than the house is worth by adding it to the mortgage. Yet another reason for being realistic.

The last few paragraphs all boil down to this. By asking the purchaser just what he is able to put down as his equity, and then what his salary is, the Estate Agent can tell immediately if the willing purchaser is going to be able to complete the purchase. In the words of the phrase much used in property circles, it is not enough that a purchaser be 'willing'. He must be 'able' as well.

There is no reason why you should not be able to use the same system as the Estate Agent, checking the status of your purchaser for yourself.

Obviously, there are differences. You must be prepared to ask what are very personal and private questions and some people may be much less forthcoming to a private person than to an Agent. The Agent is a professional man whose discretion may be relied on. It may not be true in all cases but people accept the idea much more readily than you would imagine.

Equally, you may yourself be nervous when it comes to the point of actually asking such personal questions. The only reply to this is that you simply cannot afford the wasted time that will result if your purchaser is a non starter.

Of course, you must always make it clear that you will treat what he tells you as being in complete confidence, and you must stick to your word.

If the embarrassment really is too much for you, or if he refuses to discuss the details with you, there is an alternative way to deal with the problem.

Ask the purchaser to call on his Solicitor and give the details to him. Your Solicitor will then discuss them with the Purchaser's and advise you accordingly. Of course, you must notify your Solicitor of these arrangements and you are advised to set a deadline by which you will want your Solicitor to have the information. Two days should suffice.

If the purchaser refuses to give you details of his finances; refuses to deal with them through his Solicitor or fails to let your Solicitor have the information, in time, then do not regard the house sold. You must be quite determined about this. People who are serious in their intentions and who really want to move, do not waste time and are quite open about their dealings. After all, it is in their own interests to be as helpful as possible.

For those who do ask questions and get answers, here are a few guides.

Having worked through the sum given earlier, and calculated the best possible mortgage; always check that the Purchaser has allowed for legal fees (and other costs connected with the move) in working out his available equity. For the average house, £800 is adequate; £1,000 should be more than enough for legal expenses.

Always ask for the name of the purchaser's Solicitor or Licensed Conveyancer (if he is using one), and give him yours (address too, of course). Note the buyer's name and address at the same time.

On any pieces of paper which are exchanged at this juncture, make sure that the phrase 'subject to contract' appears *every time*. This has always been regarded as allowing either party to withdraw, up to the time of the actual signing of the contract. At the time of writing, this view had been rather dented by certain decisions in the Courts, but, for the moment, it seems best to stick to the old system. If you are not happy about this, you can always take your Solicitor's or Licensed Conveyancer's advice.

It may seem strange to agree to a basis of sale which allows either party to withdraw but it is advisable. You never know. You yourself might be forced to change your plans.

Whatever happens, when your prospective purchaser departs, as a last point, make it quite clear to him that, in the event of your not receiving any information which you have requested; any deposit that has been promised; or of his not contacting his Solicitor or Licensed Conveyancer within two days, you reserve the right to re-offer the property, on the open market.

Two lost days are not too disastrous. However, two lost weeks could be very serious, particularly if you have been required to sign a contract for the purchase of the house to which you propose to move.

16

Instructing Your Solicitor and After

Why use a Solicitor? Do we really HAVE to have one? We have saved the Estate Agent's fee. Why not save the Solicitor's fee, as well?

That is really a whole range of questions. We will deal with them separately.

Firstly, No, you do not 'have' to instruct a Solicitor to deal with your sale. You can handle the contract yourself, if you wish. The only thing which is illegal is doing the job for someone else, for a fee, when you are not a qualified Solicitor or a Licensed Conveyancer.

Of course, it is quite legal for you to ignore your Doctor and to saw your own leg off. Legal, perhaps, but not very wise.

You may have saved the Agent's fee, yes, but that is because he provides a service which you can do for yourself. It is not really a professional service; it is more of a trade.

Of course, he may well also be a Surveyor or a Valuer and, in either capacity, he is carrying on a professional activity based on knowledge. As an Estate Agent, he is really a Broker, being paid for what he does, or, put another way, by results.

A Solicitor offers to protect your interests by the exercise of his knowledge and he backs up his work with a virtual guarantee. If he fails to do so, you can claim for your loss, either from him direct for professional negligence, or from the Law Society Indemnity Fund.

Unsatisfactory work by an Agent is much more difficult to deal with, even to prove. It is most unlikely that you would be able to claim any form of indemnity at all, although, it must be said, in fairness, that some Agents are members of various indemnity schemes. This is particularly so with those who have passed examinations and are allowed to describe themselves as Chartered Surveyors, Incorporated Auctioneers or Incorporated Valuers. The lesson to those employing an Agent, is obvious. Stick to the man who is properly qualified.

As mentioned earlier in the book, Licensed Conveyancers have to comply with the strict rules of their Association's code of conduct. If they break these rules, they will be liable to disciplinary proceedings. Also, in order to obtain a licence, they have to contribute towards a compensation fund and to subscribe to the Council for Licensed Conveyancers' indemnity insurance policy. This offers the same wide cover as that contained in the Law Society's master policy and does therefore give some protection to the client.

As soon as you have your purchaser arranged, telephone your Solicitor or Licensed Conveyancer and tell him what you have done; particularly if you have arranged for him to obtain information from the purchaser's Solicitor, as already outlined. After telephoning, write to confirm what you have told him.

He will want to know:

The name and address of the purchaser.

The name and address of his Solicitor or Licensed Conveyancer.

The agreed price.

The amount of any deposit that has been paid and whether it was subject to contract, survey or anything else.

Any arrangements that you have made on the basis outlined in the last chapter.

You can leave all the rest to him. He may well require more information, in which case, he will write and ask you for it. Eventually, he will want you to sign a contract and, a little later, a Conveyance, but you need not worry about that. He will keep you informed.

If you are also buying a house, with the intention of moving, you are best advised to use the same Solicitor for both conveyances. He will then be able to tie the two together. He is doing it all the time.

If you propose to remove shelving, or any items actually fastened to the building, ask your Solicitor if you are within your rights to do so. Even if he confirms that you are, think hard about it. Removing items of this sort can often damage plastering or woodwork. The Purchaser is entitled to expect the house to be just as he saw it originally. Repairing damage which you cause by removing things may cost you more than buying a replacement.

Quite early on in the procedure, the Solicitors will decide on a mutually convenient date as a 'Completion Date'. This is the date on which the purchaser will actually pay for and become the owner of the house.

On that day, you will cease to be owner, and, if you have not already done so, you move out. The purchaser pays, becomes owner and moves in, as soon as he wishes, thereafter.

All that need be said on this point, is this.

Do not allow the buyer to take possession before the completion date, without consulting your Solicitor. Once in possession, the buyer could, if he was so minded, delay paying you for a long time. He could even make a case that he is really a Tenant, and a protected one, at that. Avoid such a situation by not letting him in.

He may wish to measure for carpets, curtains, etc., and, if you have already moved out, he will want to borrow the key. Consult your Solicitor first, but, in any case, never let him have the key unless he signs a receipt, stating that the key is lent 'for the purposes of viewing, only'.

When you do move out, leave the house clean and take away all rubbish. You would be amazed how much dirt and unwanted old junk, is left by Vendors. If you do not want it, is it likely that the buyer of the house, will? Play the game – get rid of it. He will have enough to worry about, just moving his furniture in.

Leave a forwarding address with the buyer. If you are wise, you will have arranged with the Post Office to redirect your mail, anyway, but letters do slip through the net. It is better to be safe than sorry. In any case, it shows some degree of good faith to the Purchaser.

Well, that is it. We hope that you will be happy in your new home, and that things have gone smoothly. If they did not then you can console yourself that you are not alone. The guidance given here will enable you to control the situation as far as possible but there is always the risk of influences over which you can have no control.

Changes in government policy; mortgage famine; wars; plagues etc., can make the house seller's efforts doubly difficult but, if it is any comfort, the Professional is only marginally in a better position to deal with such problems.

For all that, the advice given in these pages still stands. If you have any doubt about any aspect of house selling; if you doubt your own ability to handle the matter,

GO TO AN ESTATE AGENT.

Appendix 1
Useful Addresses

The Royal Institution of Chartered Surveyors, 12 Great George Street, London, SW1P 3AD

The Law Society, 113 Chancery Lane, London, WC2A 1PL

The Housing Corporation, Maple House, 149 Tottenham Court Road, London, W1P 0BN

The Incorporated Society of Valuers & Auctioneers, 3 Cadogan Gate, London, SW1X 0AF

The National House Building Council, 58 Portland Place, London, W1N 4BU

The Land Registry, Land Charges Department, Burrington Way, Plymouth, Devon.

The Citizens Advice Bureau. The address of the local CAB office is almost always on the notice board of public announcements, in the Post Office.

Appendix 2

Mortgage Repayments
The figure given represents the monthly payment for every £1,000 borrowed.

Length of Mortgage	Interest rates payable						
	9%	10%	11%	12%	13%	14%	15%
15 years	£10.34	£10.96	£11.59	£12.24	£12.90	£13.57	£14.25
20 "	9.13	9.79	10.47	11.16	11.86	12.58	13.31
25 "	8.49	9.19	9.90	10.62	11.37	12.12	12.89
30 "	8.12	8.84	9.59	10.35	11.12	11.90	12.69

Notes
1. In the majority of cases the interest paid will be reduced by the effect of MIRAS (see page 76). As interest rates vary, and so do income tax levels, the figures are given gross and should be reduced by figures that the Building Society Manager will be able to tell you.

2. Some Building Societies calculate interest due more frequently than others and this can cause variations in the monthly repayments from those given above. For practical purposes the variations will be small and the figures given are accurate enough to allow you to make your initial calculations.

3. Readers with their own electronic calculators can work out a close approximation of their mortgage repayments for any combinations of loan, interest rate and repayment period by use of the following formula:

For *annual* repayment $\dfrac{Lr(1+r)^n}{(1+r)^n - 1}$

Where L is the amount of the initial loan in pounds, n is the number of years and r is the rate percent compound interest per annum expressed as a decimal (e.g. 9% is 0·09, $13\frac{1}{4}$% is 0·1325, etc.). The repayments are equal annual payments. After n payments, the loan and interest is paid off.

Monthly repayments would each be about one twelfth of the annual repayments, but this can vary a little according to the way in which the Building Society charges interest.

Appendix 3

Premium Payments

To qualify for Premium Payment you must

(*a*) Have been a Tenant of the Society or company, for five years.

(*b*) Have paid all charges regularly.

Also,

(*c*) The property must have been let at a higher rent than you were paying. And,

(*d*) The security amount (explained later) must not prevent payment.

The Payment comes in two parts.

(*a*) The Basic Amount. This is the sum of those charges which you have paid and which have gone towards paying off the Company's mortgage. After five years, for example, this would be 1 per cent of the original Capital Value of the property.

(*b*) The Valuation Amount. If the house has been let for a higher rent than you were paying, then the Capital Value will have increased at the same rate. You may qualify for a share of this sum. After five years, this would be 50 per cent of the increase.

Whatever the Premium Payment may be, it will be limited to the 'Security Amount'. This is the amount by which the new Capital Value exceeds the Mortgage still outstanding on the house.'

INDEX

OUR PUBLISHING POLICY

HOW WE CHOOSE

Our policy is to consider every deserving manuscript and we can give special editorial help where an author is an authority on his subject but an inexperienced writer. We are rigorously selective in the choice of books we publish. We set the highest standards of editorial quality and accuracy. This means that a *Paperfront* is easy to understand and delightful to read. Where illustrations are necessary to convey points of detail, these are drawn up by a subject specialist artist from our panel.

HOW WE KEEP PRICES LOW

We aim for the big seller. This enables us to order enormous print runs and achieve the lowest price for you. Unfortunately, this means that you will not find in the *Paperfront* list any titles on obscure subjects of minority interest only. These could not be printed in large enough quantities to be sold for the low price at which we offer this series. We sell almost all our *Paperfronts* at the same unit price. This saves a lot of fiddling about in our clerical departments and helps us to give you world-beating value. Under this system, the longer titles are offered at a price which we believe to be unmatched by any publisher in the world.

OUR DISTRIBUTION SYSTEM

Because of the competitive price, and the rapid turnover, *Paperfronts* are possibly the most profitable line a bookseller can handle. They are stocked by the best bookshops all over the world. It may be that your bookseller has run out of stock of a particular title. If so, he can order more from us at any time—we have a fine reputation for 'same day' despatch, and we supply any order, however small (even a single copy), to any bookseller who has an account with us. We prefer you to buy from your bookseller, as this reminds him of the strong underlying public demand for *Paperfronts*. Members of the public who live in remote places, or who are housebound, or whose local bookseller is unco-operative, can order direct from us by post.

FREE

If you would like an up-to-date list of all paperfront titles currently available, send a stamped self-addressed envelope to
ELLIOT RIGHT WAY BOOKS, BRIGHTON RD.,
LOWER KINGSWOOD, SURREY, U.K.